End Times

CHURCH DECEPTION

ARE YOU READY?

End Times
CHURCH DECEPTION

TODD PERLA M.D.

WINEPRESS WP PUBLISHING

WinePress Publishing (PO Box 428, Enumclaw, WA 98022) functions only as book publisher. As such, the ultimate design, content, editorial accuracy, and views expressed or implied in this work are those of the author.

ISBN 13: 978-1-57921-921-5
ISBN 10: 1-57921-921-7
Library of Congress Catalog Card Number: 2007932451

To our persecuted brethren throughout the world:
May God continue to give you the strength to endure. May organizations
like Voice of the Martyrs be empowered to serve as an advocate for you.
May we intercede in prayer and identify with our persecuted brethren
throughout the world, as we may soon follow in their path.

CONTENTS

Introduction: When Will the Church Be Raptured? ix

Part 1: Refuting the Fallacies Surrounding Belief in a Pretribulation Rapture

1. Fallacy 1: "Christians Never Experience the Wrath of God" 1
2. Fallacy 2: "The Church Saints Are Not Mentioned Between Revelation 4 and 19" 7
3. Fallacy 3: "The Seven Churches Reference Literal Eras of Church History". 17
4. Fallacy 4: "Christ Comes as a 'Thief in the Night' to All" 21
5. Fallacy 5: "The Church and the Holy Spirit Are the 'Restraining Force' of 2 Thessalonians 2" 25
6. Fallacy 6: "The Seventh Trumpet and the Last Trumpet Call of God Occur in Two Distinct Contexts" 29
7. Fallacy 7: "The Age of the Gentiles Ends Sometime Before the Tribulation". 33
8. Fallacy 8: "The Two Resurrections Occur Simultaneously" 35

Part 2: Timing Is Everything in Clearing the Deception

9. Multiple References to the Raptured Saints in Revelation Verify the Timing 41
10. The Wedding Supper of the Lamb 49
11. Timing of the Battle of Armageddon 53

12. The Tribulation Thirty-Day Time Discrepancy
    Clearly Solved 59
13. What the Psalms Say about the Timing of the Rapture 65
14. What the Prophet Isaiah Said about the
    Timing of the Rapture 69
15. What Jesus Said about the Timing of the Rapture 73
16. The New Testament and Timing of the Rapture 75

Part 3: Major People and Events of the End Times
17. The Origins of the Antichrist 91
18. The Antichrist and the Four Horses of the Apocalypse 97
19. The False Prophet 103
20. The Two Witnesses 109
21. The Trumpets 115
22 The Bowl Judgments 123
23. The Last Babylon 129
24. Israel in End-Times Bible Prophecy 135
25. The Great End-Times Revival 151
26. The Great Ingathering 155
27. The Millennial Kingdom 163
28. The Millennial Kingdom 173
29. The Eternal State 185

Postscript What Should We Do to Prepare for Christ's Return? . . . 189

Timeline of Final Events 202

INTRODUCTION:
WHEN WILL THE CHURCH BE RAPTURED?

From the time of Christ's ascension into heaven, Christians have eagerly anticipated his return, many expecting it any day, hoping it would occur during their lifetimes.

Many consider that the escalation of earthquakes, hurricanes, tsunamis, and other devastating weather patterns all over the world, as well as the rise of famines, terrorist threats, and "wars and rumors of wars" gives support that we are near the time of the end.

These signs may indeed be significant, but the most important signpost for the beginning of the end is the nation of Israel. We witnessed Israel's becoming a nation again in 1948—in a single day, as predicted in the Bible. (See Isa. 66:8.)

Most biblical scholars believe Israel symbolizes the "fig tree" Jesus talked about in Matthew 24:32–33: "Now learn this lesson from the fig tree: As soon as its twigs get tender and its leaves come out, you know that summer is near. Even so, when you see all these things, you know that it is near, right at the door." (See also Luke 21:29–36.) The "fig tree" Israel has definitely "sprouted leaves" through its growth and prosperity as a nation, but Israel has not blossomed yet, as it has not had any large-scale Jewish conversions to Christ. We must remember Jesus did then say when the fig bears leaves, "this generation will certainly not pass away until all these things have happened" (Matt. 24:34). So if we have this prophecy right, we may indeed be living in that last generation, a view many Bible scholars hold.

In more recent times, many other prophecies concerning the nation Israel have been fulfilled, setting the stage for the end times to unfold. Chapter 24 includes more discussion about these specific prophecies.

For much of my Christian life I've believed in a pretribulation rapture. It's a comfortable belief, since none of us wants to experience the horrors of the tribulation period, with all its pain and suffering. After extensively researching the topic in the Scriptures, however, I'm convinced that the pretribulation view of the rapture is not the truth. In this book we will discuss more than one hundred scriptural evidences that refute a pretribulation rapture doctrine, which, I trust will clearly put to rest this false teaching.

From the time of the apostles up until around the mid-1870s, the predominant evangelical theology was a rapture at the second coming of Christ near the end of tribulation. An Anglican minister named John Nelson Darby was the first to present a pretribulation rapture view in America, a view that was initially rejected by the seminaries as heresy. But when Darby partnered with Scofield, who developed Bible study notes the seminary students used to help study efficiently for their exams, this doctrine sneaked in the back door. Darby's doctrine on the end times slowly but surely became the predominant view, and now more than 90 percent of American Christians believe this is the correct view (April 1995, Gallup poll).

So, who's right? Are we discounting eighteen hundred years of church scholarship and leadership? Are the writings of early church fathers such as Barnabas, Clement, and Justin Martyr off base? Was the Council of Nicea (A.D. 325) in error when they declared as orthodox doctrine a post-tribulation rapture?

Some pretribulation rapture proponents say the mainline church has been wrong in the past with doctrinal issues, so it's not wise to base much on review of the history of church doctrine. The same skeptics refer to the times of Constantine, when the official religion of the Roman Empire was made Christian and the generally accepted interpretation of the book of Revelation was changed from a literal to a purely symbolic one. Constantine promoted this view, which rejected a literal thousand-year millennial kingdom, because, many speculate, he felt threatened by the thought of a millennium kingdom that could be greater than the Roman Empire. It was a purely political move, and had nothing to do with a better understanding of the Scriptures.

Prominent church leaders in the more recent past—Martin Luther, John Calvin, John Knox, Charles Spurgeon, George Whitefield, Jonathan Edwards, William Tyndale, and John Wesley—also preached the truth of the rapture at the second coming of Christ near the end of tribulation. Many Christians in America today would be surprised to know about the beliefs of these respected men of faith, but preachers in America avoid referencing these men when preaching on the topic of the rapture. Ironically, these same modern-day preachers will often quote Luther, Calvin, Wesley, and others when discussing almost any other aspect of the Christian faith.

Given Christianity's rich history of orthodox belief, why are there so many erroneous teachings on the end times? I can think of several reasons.

First, telling people they need to accept Jesus Christ as Savior, and then that they will likely be decapitated or captured, or need to flee into hiding during the upcoming tribulation period would not be a very popular message. The pretribulation rapture belief is a much more pleasant stance. Many church members desire what "their itching ears want to hear" (2 Tim. 4:3). We like the health, wealth, and prosperity doctrine preached in many churches throughout America today and prefer to avoid the topic of persecution altogether.

Second, many preachers are simply ignorant of the truth. They have not studied end-times Scriptures well enough to be enlightened to the truth, so they just regurgitate what they've read in books or heard others say. Ignorance is no excuse, however; preachers are called to a higher standard as teachers of the Word (Jas. 3:1). They will be held accountable before God for this error.

Third, some preachers are unwilling to admit they've been preaching false doctrine on the end times—perhaps because of pride or fear of losing members, financial support, or seminary and denominational affiliations. Sadly, they would rather set up their congregations for "tribulation tragedy" and lead their very own "sheep to slaughter," rather than repent and tell them the truth about this false doctrine.

Fortunately, there are a few prominent preachers and authors in America today who *do* preach the truth about the rapture and that Christians will experience the tribulation. These men include R. C. Sproul, Hank Hanegraaff, and Marvin Rosenthal. Rosenthal was once a leading proponent of a pretribulation rapture, but he recently changed his stance and wrote a book on the issue titled *The Pre-Wrath Rapture of the Church*. Robert Van Kampen and Hank Hanegraaff have also recently written books supporting the rapture at the second coming of Christ, near the end of the tribulation.

In this book I hope to build on what these men have written, as well as add unique perspectives and more detail on many aspects of the end times as supported by the Scriptures. I firmly believe that a more literal interpretation of the Bible is crucial to giving us the key to the end-times prophecies. When we analyze and study Scripture, we should first take a "face-value" or commonsense approach. We should also factor in the context of the writing, the culture of the time, and the original Hebrew, Aramaic, or Greek language used. We should also look for metaphors, similes, and other literary devices. Of course, some passages are not meant to be interpreted literally, and doing so would lead to error. If we find the literal interpretation of a specific passage or verse in balance with of the entirety of the Bible, however, and with no apparent contradictions, then we are probably on the right path of reasoning.

Though denominations have their place, I use the Bible for my guide, and not some doctrinal statement. Though I've studied these end-times Scriptures in great detail, I don't use language intended to intimidate or impress. You don't need a seminary degree to understand what's written here. I use a similar approach with my medical practice. Though I could use sophisticated medical jargon when talking with patients, I realize it is best to use understandable terms so they can clearly understand the diagnosis, treatment, and prognosis. In this book I make a clear diagnosis of the poor state of the spiritual health of America and its churches as a whole. The necessary treatment involves a reality check, repentance, and a dose of sound biblical truth. If our condition does not quickly change, we will not be physically, psychologically, or spiritually prepared for what is ahead. Many of us will become spiritual casualties who will participate in the "great falling away" that will occur in the last days. Yes, we may individually still get to heaven in our current condition, but if we don't get the right medicine quickly, we will suffer much in the coming days and will lose an abundance of eternal reward.

Knowing the truth about the end-times prophecies should give encouragement to the tribulation saints. The book of Revelation will be a blessing to those who understand: "Blessed is the one who reads the words of this prophecy, and blessed are those who hear it and take to heart what is written in it, because the time is near" (Rev. 1:3). Also, the saints who know their end times will likely be the "wise" mentioned in Daniel 11:33, who "will instruct many." They will be prepared for what's ahead. Though their world will be harsh and nightmarish, the day of their relief and glorification will come.

Christ Jesus is coming, and he will be revealed to all in his great glory! He will not come silently or in humility this second time around, but in great power and majesty to judge the rebellious world for their ungodliness and to rescue his faithful children.

PART 1
REFUTING THE FALLACIES SURROUNDING
BELIEF IN A PRETRIBULATION RAPTURE

Chapter 1

Of the many reasons pretribulation-rapture proponents give to defend their position, the most popular involves the belief that the "wrath of God" occurs during the tribulation and Christians are not subject to God's wrath, therefore they must not be around during this time. At first glance, this appears to be a reasonable argument. But what about those people who will be born again during the tribulation? They'll certainly be on hand to experience God's wrath.

1 Thessalonians 5:9

The most quoted verse pertaining to God's wrath as a defense for a pretribulation rapture is 1 Thessalonians 5:9: "For God did not appoint us to suffer wrath but to receive salvation through our Lord Jesus Christ." I agree that this verse does imply that Christians will not suffer the wrath that comes after "the day of the Lord," which is the second coming of Christ. In other words, God's final fury, unleashed in the last days of the tribulation, will not be experienced by believers. However, the focus of the verse here is more that all believers will inherit salvation in heaven, versus eternal condemnation and punishment in "gehenna," or what some may call "hell."

The Bible is quite clear on the fate of those who reject Christ:

- "The wrath of God is being revealed from heaven against all godlessness and wickedness of men who suppress the truth by their wickedness" (Rom. 1:18).

- "All of us also lived among them at one time, gratifying the cravings of our sinful nature and following its desires and thoughts. Like the rest, we were by nature objects of wrath" (Eph. 2:3).
- "Whoever believes in the Son has eternal life, but whoever rejects the Son will not see life, for God's wrath remains on him" (John 3:36).
- See also Romans 2:5–8 and Romans 5:9.

Christians are spared the wrath of God in regard to the wrath of gehenna and the wrath that will come after the second coming of Christ, but are God's people spared wrath while they live out their lives here on earth? Perhaps we need to shift our paradigm on the subject of God's wrath.

God's Wrath in the Old Testament

Psalm 38:1–3 says, "O Lord, do not rebuke me in your anger or discipline me in your wrath. For your arrows have pierced me, and your hand has come down upon me. Because of your wrath there is no health in my body, my bones have no soundness because of my sin." Here David, through inspiration of God, tells us God's wrath came down on him because of his sin. (See also Pss. 88:7; 88:16; 89:46; 90:7, 9, 11, 15; 110:5.) There are numerous other Old Testament examples—some of them involving plagues, diseases, and even death—of God's wrath against his people. (See Ex. 33:35; Num. 12:9–10; 16:1–50; Deut. 9:8; 11:16; 25:1–18; 32:39; Josh. 7:1–26; 1 Sam. 2:27–4:18; 2 Sam. 24:1, 13–15; Job 19:21; Isa. 10:25; Ezek. 5:16; 6:12; Amos 3:2; Mic. 7:9.)

God's Wrath in the New Testament

Some may say God's wrath is different in the Old Testament than it is in the New Testament. Malachi 3:6 says, "I the LORD do not change." And Hebrews 13:8 says, "Jesus Christ is the same yesterday and today and forever." Does God hate sin any less in the New Testament than he does in the Old Testament? Recall the story of Ananias and Sapphira (Acts 5:1–11), and see how the wrath of God was displayed against his own people for their sin. Yes, their (and our) sin is forgiven, but there are still consequences to that sin. Paul wrote to the Corinthians regarding their abuse of the Lord's Supper, saying, "That is why many among you are weak and sick, and a number of you have fallen asleep [died]" (1 Cor. 11:30). Other passages underscore this truth:

- "For it is time for judgment to begin with the family of God; and if it begins with us, what will the outcome be for those who do not obey the gospel of God?" (1 Pet. 4:17).
- "So when you, a mere man, pass judgment on them and yet do the same things, do you think you will escape God's judgment?" (Rom. 2:3).
- "Do not judge, or you too will be judged. For in the same way you judge others, you will be judged, and with the measure you use, it will be measured to you" (Matt. 7:1–2).
- "But if our unrighteousness brings out God's righteousness more clearly, what shall we say? That God is unjust in bringing his wrath on us?" (Rom. 3:5).
- "When we are judged by the Lord, we are being disciplined so that we will not be condemned with the world" (1 Cor. 11:32).

Although Christians are judged for sin while we live out our lives here on earth, fortunately, our sins have been forgiven and we will not face eternal condemnation.

The Objects of God's Tribulation Wrath

Though the Bible clearly shows the wrath of God can be manifested against sin in the lives of Christians, I still believe that the wrath unleashed by God during the tribulation is directed toward the unsaved, the worldly systems, and Satan and his demons. The tribulation judgments of God are not specifically documented as "wrath" until the sixth seal (Rev. 6:17), and in conjunction with the seventh trumpet judgment (Rev. 11:18), and with the first bowl judgment (Rev. 16:2). God's most severe wrath occurs after the second coming, a time described as the "hour of testing" or "hour of judgment," where the "earth dwellers" will be tested or judged by God, and yet will not repent and be saved. The rapture of the church occurs before this "wrath" is poured out on the earth.

The Wrath of Man

While Christians will escape the majority of God's wrath during the tribulation, they will surely suffer the wrath of man. Luke 21:23–24 says, "How dreadful it will be in those days for pregnant women and nursing mothers! There will be great distress in the land and wrath against this people. They will fall by the sword and will be taken as prisoners to all the nations." Revelation 13:7 talks about the Antichrist having power to "make war against the saints and to conquer them." Daniel 11:36 says the Antichrist will be successful until "the time of wrath is completed, for what has been determined will take place."

Supernatural Protection

Even if one believes that the wrath of God is unleashed throughout the tribulation, a church rapture at the second coming of Christ would not necessarily mean that these end-times Christians would directly experience the tribulation wrath. God will supernaturally protect his people, despite their presence on the earth as the tribulation judgments of God are being unveiled.

Revelation 7:3–8 mentions the "144,000" who have a "seal on their foreheads" prior to the angels of judgment being allowed to "harm the land and the sea." This reference is probably associated with the time immediately prior to the first three trumpets being sounded, as these judgments line up exactly with those described in Revelation 8:6–11. Also, Revelation 9:4 says those with the "seal of God" were spared the fifth trumpet judgment of scorpion stings. From these specific references, we can infer that God's people are spared all the other trumpet judgments. Revelation 16:2 discusses the first bowl judgment and how it will be specifically for those who "had the mark of the beast." There is no mention of any of the bowl judgments affecting the elect of God, because they are raptured prior to these judgments.

Bible history gives us similar analogies of God's people being supernaturally protected while the wrath of God is being unleashed all around them. For example, the Israelites were living in Egypt when the Nile was turned to blood, and when the other plagues (gnats, flies, boils, and so forth) occurred. Nowhere does the Scripture mention these judgments directly harmed the Israelites, even though they lived side by side with the Egyptians (Ex. 5–11). God supernaturally protected his people, just as the tribulation saints will also be protected against his divine wrath. Think, too, of how God spared Noah and his family from the flood (Gen. 6–9), how he protected the nation of Israel from starvation through Joseph in Egypt (Gen. 41–47), how he sustained his prophet Elijah amid drought and famine through a tiny stream and a few ravens (1 Kings 17).

God's history, so to speak, of protecting his people doesn't end in the Old Testament. In the New Testament, an angel appeared to Joseph in a dream, instructing him to take Mary and Jesus to Egypt to escape Herod's anger (Matt. 2). Peter was miraculously released from prison by an angel (Acts 12), and Paul suffered no harm when a poisonous snake bit him (Acts 28).

Whatever your view on the timing of the rapture, the issue of wrath isn't a factor. Christians are not exempt from experiencing God's wrath, but the tribulation wrath of God is not directed toward God's elect. Instead, it is focused on the ungodly and the systems of evil that have set themselves up against God.

Chapter 2

M any verses in Revelation 4–19 reference the church collectively as "the saints" and the "great multitude" in purely symbolic or metaphorical terms. Perhaps the churches aren't named as specific churches in later chapters because most Christians have had to flee the organized apostate churches of the last days, or have been captured, or have died and are in heaven. It could also be that, after addressing the churches individually in Revelation 2:1–3:22, the church saints are subsequently addressed as a single body of believers, the true remnant from among the apostate churches of the end times. No matter the reason, the reality is that in no way are the church saints silent within these chapters. For example, Revelation 6:9–11 tells of the martyred saints in heaven asking God how much longer it will be until their blood can be avenged. Certainly many of these martyrs are from the church age. Verse 11 says, "they were told to wait a little longer, until the number of their fellow servants and brothers who were to be killed as they had been was completed." God still had some more Christians to be martyred during the tribulation. It's interesting to note that the "souls" of these martyred saints do not have resurrected bodies, because the rapture has not yet occurred. This fact is clearly a contradiction to a pretribulation rapture, because those saints would have had resurrected bodies if the rapture had already occurred.

Revelation 7

Revelation 7 starts in a setting near the beginning of the tribulation and is an answer to the question asked at the end of chapter 6: "For the great day of their wrath has come, and who can stand?" (Rev. 6:17). The people discussed in chapter 7 are those who will stand at the second coming of Christ, because they are the redeemed—both the 144,000, the Jewish contingent of the "great multitude" which, as a whole consists of representation from "every nation" and "standing before the throne and in front of the Lamb" (Rev. 7:9). These same blessed people are called the "bride of Christ" in Revelation 19:6–9, which we'll discuss later. Certainly the church saints are well represented in the great multitude and bride of Christ.

The 144,000

The 144,000 are the Jewish male evangelists who are converted early in the tribulation and preach the gospel throughout the world. They are given a "seal" (Rev. 7:3), so that the later trumpet judgments against the land, sea, trees, and the unsaved don't affect them. The Jewish prophetic timeline referenced in Daniel 9:20–27 has been at a standstill, until the last seven years of tribulation begins, when the Antichrist orchestrates a peace treaty between the nation Israel and their enemies around the world. It would make sense that the 144,000 Jewish evangelists get saved somewhere near the beginning of the tribulation, as the Jewish timeline starts back up at that time. Because the conversion of the 144,000 occurs before the second coming of Christ, they are participants in the rapture. Evidence for their participation in the rapture is seen in Revelation 14:3–5:

> And they sang a new song before the throne and before the four living creatures and the elders. No one could learn the song except the 144,000 who had been redeemed from the earth. These are those who did not defile themselves with women, for they kept themselves pure. They follow the Lamb wherever he goes. They were purchased from among men and offered as firstfruits to

God and the Lamb. No lie was found in their mouths; they are blameless.

Notice that the 144,000 are redeemed "from the earth" and are "firstfruits." In other places in the New Testament, both Jesus and the Gentile saints are called "firstfruits" (1 Cor. 15:23; Rom. 8:23) Farmers always harvest the "firstfruits" initially, followed by the general harvest at a later date. The firstfruits harvest would be analogous to the rapture of the church and the general harvest would represent those gathered in at the end of the millennial kingdom. So these 144,000 are the firstfruits from among the Jews that convert to Christ.

The Great Multitude

The "great multitude" (Rev. 7:9) represents believers from all Jewish and Gentile nations who are seen in their post-rapture glorified bodies. If Jews were not included in the great multitude, verse 9 would not have specifically said "from every nation, tribe, people and language." Revelation 7:3 discusses the "seal on the foreheads of the servants of our God" in discussing the 144,000 Jewish converts. Though the great multitude is not discussed in this verse, clearly they are also "servants of God" and would be expected to have the "seal of God." Since the great multitude involves a number that "no one could count," that may be why they are not specifically mentioned there in verse 9 along with the 144,000.

Most pretribulation rapture believers claim the great multitude is made up of those saved during the tribulation, after the rapture of the church. They convert to Christ during the tribulation, through the witness of the 144,000 and the "two witnesses" (Rev. 11). For this to be true, the great multitude, who are in heaven in this scene, would have had to have been martyred for their faith; otherwise they would still be living as mortals on the earth and not be seen in heaven at this point. But Revelation 7:14 clearly states, "These are they who have come out of the great tribulation; they have washed their robes and made them white in the blood of the Lamb." There's no reference to martyrdom here, as their robes were washed with the blood of the Lamb, not their own blood. The martyrs throughout the history of the church are referenced in Revelation 6:9–11, with many tribulation martyrs included in this group. I firmly believe the great multitude mentioned in Revelation 7:9–14 represent believers who entered the tribulation, including those new believers who convert after the tribulation begins. Notice that the 144,000 came "out of the great tribulation," because the church is raptured during the great tribulation period, and not before the tribulation even begins.

The reference to the magnitude of saints involved in the great multitude refutes a pretribulation rapture. The number implied is so enormous that "no one could count, from every nation, tribe, people and language" (Rev. 7:9). In my mind, this equates to millions or billions of people, a group so large that no person would live long enough to count its members. There is no scriptural support for such a large number of new believers coming to the Lord during the tribulation (prior to the second coming of Christ) to qualify for such a great multitude. During this time there will be tremendous persecution; the cost of being a true Christian will be great. That is probably why there is a great "falling away" prophesied during the tribulation. There are many scripture references predicting a great apostasy or time of generalized unbelief during the tribulation, such as what occurred during the pre-flood times of Noah. Amos 8:11 discusses a "famine of hearing the words of the Lord" during the tribulation, so how could millions be saved during this time? There is no support for a massive revival in the tribulation until after the second coming of Christ. Now, if the church is raptured before the tribulation even begins, then there could not possibly be billions of Christians around to be consistent with the great multitude without causing a contradiction in the Scriptures. However, if the church is around during the tribulation, then there is support for such a large number of Christians being raptured out of the tribulation. Another reference to similarly sized multitudes is found in Daniel 12:2, which speaks of the "multitudes who sleep in the dust of the earth" and how their bodies resurrect to everlasting life (in the first resurrection) or everlasting contempt (in the second resurrection). We can definitely agree that the number of Christians throughout the whole history of time is a very large number, which no one can count.

Revelation 9:4

In Revelation 9:4, people who had the "seal of God on their foreheads" were spared the sting of the scorpions involved with the fifth trumpet judgment. Those sealed are the church saints, or the great multitude, as they will be spared the wrath of this judgment. This is again similar to how God protected the Israelites from the plagues he sent on the Egyptians during the time of Moses. God knows his people, and will spare them his tribulation wrath.

Revelation 11:15–18

In conjunction with the seventh trumpet in Revelation 11:15, "The time has come for judging the dead, and for rewarding your servants the prophets and your saints and those who reverence your name, both small and great—and for destroying those who destroy the earth" (Rev. 11:18). Clearly this is the judging of the saints. (The destroying of the earth will start with the "hour of testing" at the second coming and after the rapture, and will be discussed in later chapters. See Rev. 3:3; 14:7; 18:10; 17:19 for other references to the "hour.")

Revelation 12

Revelation 12 is a very symbolic chapter that goes back in time all the way to the fall of Lucifer and one-third of the angels who rebelled in heaven (Rev. 12:7–9). It then takes us up through the tribulation, with the church included in the symbolism.

In Revelation 12:1 the woman "clothed with the sun, with the moon under her feet and a crown of twelve stars on her head" represents the nation Israel. (See also Gen. 37:9; Ps. 89:35.) The woman Israel gives birth to a son (Jesus) in verse 5, who is "snatched up to God" at the resurrection. In verse 6 the woman flees into the desert to a place prepared for her protection for 1,260 days. This place of refuge is Petra or Bozrah, which we will discuss in more detail later. Revelation 12:7–9 discusses a second battle in heaven, but this time Satan loses complete access to heaven with his defeat. (See Rev. 9:1–2.) Then verses 10–12 describe the scene in heaven, where the martyred saints—many of whom are from the church age—proclaim that the millennium kingdom of

Christ is about to start, because Satan is released in full fury upon the earth, as the "time is short." These martyred saints probably witnessed the second angelic rebellion, since that's how they knew the end was near and their blood would finally be avenged. (See Rev. 6:9–11.) In verses 13–16, Satan is again trying to demolish the woman, who is carried by an eagle (representing God) to a place in the desert, where she is protected for three-and-a-half years. Then, in verse 17, the saints are again referenced as the woman's "offspring," whom Satan tries to make war against, as he cannot kill the elect Jews, who are protected by God in the desert area of Petra. These "offspring" could very well include Gentiles who are tribulation saints living in the second half of the tribulation, and they could include elect Jews who did not leave Jerusalem at the "abomination of desolation" (Matt. 24:15–21). Those Jews who don't heed that warning convert to Christ and suffer persecution (Matt. 10:17–23). Some of the offspring are caught and put in jail or ultimately killed for their faith. Others will flee to self-imposed exile. (See the postscript "What Should We Do to Prepare for Christ's Return?" for more information on self-imposed exile or captivity.)

Revelation 13

The saints are clearly referenced in Revelation 13:7, where the Antichrist makes "war against the saints . . . to conquer them." Then, in verses 9–10, the saints are given two proactive options: to enter into self-imposed captivity (or exile) or to fight the Antichrist and be killed.

> He who has an ear, let him hear.
>
> If anyone is to go into captivity, into captivity he will go. If anyone is to be killed with the sword, with the sword he will be killed.
>
> This calls for patient endurance and faithfulness on the part of the saints.

Incidentally, in the book of Revelation, the phrase "He who has an ear, let him hear" is only used to call attention to instruction or exhortation directed toward the church. Thus, verse 10 is clearly directed toward all church believers, without mention to the churches individually, because they have been addressed previously in Revelation 2:1–3:22, and the general calling is for all church believers. (More specifics on this in the Postscript.)

Revelation 14:12–16

The church saints are again mentioned in Revelation 14:12, calling for them to have "patient endurance" and to "remain faithful to Jesus." Verse 13 says, "Blessed are the dead who die in the Lord from now on." These tribulation saints are blessed in the millennium kingdom, where the "beheaded" and other martyrs for the faith will have special significance as judges (Rev. 20:4). It's not clearly evident if the martyrs referenced here correlate with the start of the tribulation or a specific time within the tribulation. It may be that the tribulation is so terrible for the saints that their eternal reward will be so much greater, because they did not deny Christ or "shrink from death" (Rev. 12:11).

Revelation 14:14–16 again backtracks to the rapture, when one "like a son of man" having a "sickle in his hand" is told by "another angel . . . 'Take your sickle and reap, because the time to reap has come.'" Those reaped are church saints at the time of the rapture.

Revelation 15

Revelation 15 depicts the scene in heaven after the rapture and before the last seven bowl judgments are to be poured out to complete God's wrath on all the earth. The "sea of glass mixed with fire" (verse 2) symbolizes the sea of humanity when the fiery wrath of God is unleashed on it. Those standing beside the sea are the church saints who are raptured, as they "had been victorious over the beast and his image and over the number of his name." They had not received the mark of the Beast, which was on the right hand or forehead—the number 666—of those destined for hell.

Revelation 16

Revelation 16 is devoid of the church in symbolism or direct representation because the church is raptured out at this point, before the seven bowl judgments are poured out on all the unsaved of humanity who remain on planet earth. The bowl judgments are part of the "hour of testing" for the earth. This chapter is also devoid of heavenly scenes, where we might anticipate hearing from the saints.

Revelation 17

Revelation 17 includes a great deal of symbolism, and it backtracks to the beginning of the tribulation. The "great prostitute" in verse 1 is the last religious system of the end times that is established in the first half of the tribulation. The religious system "prostituted" itself for money and power. It is seen "sitting on a scarlet beast" in verse 3, so the Antichrist is a critical advocate for this system of religion.

Verse 6 indicates that the church saints were killed by this religious system. "I saw that the woman was drunk with the blood of the saints, the blood of those who bore testimony to Jesus." It is important to restate that this "prostitute" (false religious system) is in place in the first half of the tribulation, and therefore the persecution of Christians would be projected to start early in the tribulation.

The church saints are again mentioned as "faithful followers" of Christ in verse 14, who will win the final war against the Antichrist in the battle of Armageddon.

Revelation 19

After the long discussion in chapter 18 on the "hour of testing" and ultimate judgment of Babylon, the saints are referenced again in Revelation 19:6 as the "great multitude" shouting praises to God in heaven.

Revelation 19:7–9 talks of the "bride" dressed in fine linen, which represents the righteous saints who have been judged and given glorified bodies. Verse 9 says, "Blessed are those who are invited to the wedding supper of the Lamb!" The timing of the "wedding supper" clearly occurs in close association with the rapture, when the saints are glorified. One would have a hard time explaining a pretribulation rapture, where the bride and groom would be waiting seven years after their union for the wedding supper to occur.

Revelation 19:11–17 portrays Jesus riding a "white horse" with his "armies of heaven" in support for the final battle of Armageddon, in which the Beast and False Prophet are defeated and thrown into the "fiery lake." Those armies of heaven include the raptured church believers who come with Jesus at the end of the tribulation to defeat the enemy.

Revelation 20

Revelation 20:4–6 mentions "thrones" on which the church saints sit and are given authority to judge the peoples of the world during the millennial period. In verse 11 the church saints are seen witnessing the "great white throne" judgment of all nonbelievers, at the end of the millennium kingdom and after the final rebellion.

Revelation 21

Revelation 21 again backtracks to the creation of the "new heaven and new earth" that occurs at the end of the tribulation. The church is called the "bride" in both verses 2 and 9—but in two different settings. Verse 2 refers to the time of the "eternal state," that starts when the "bride" and "the new Jerusalem" come from heaven down to earth level. Then verse 9 backtracks to just after the second coming of Christ, when heaven is attached to the "great mountain" of Mount Zion, during the millennial kingdom and before the "eternal state." (We will discuss these two different settings for the "bride" in subsequent chapters.)

Revelation 22

In Revelation 22:12–13 Jesus says, "Behold, I am coming soon! My reward is with me, and I will give to everyone according to what he has done. I am the Alpha and the Omega, the First and the Last, the Beginning and the End." Jesus is addressing the church, telling them his second coming is associated with the "reward" of the rapture. This will be a glorious time for his church and will be the end of time for them, as they will be in the "eternal state." Clearly the second coming is associated with the "end of the ages" and rapture. There is no reference to this occurring seven years earlier, prior to the start of tribulation.

Revelation 22:16–17 is the last reference to the church, and what a fitting conclusion! Jesus says to John, "I, Jesus, have sent my angel to give you this testimony for the churches" (verse 16). Why would the angel give the testimony *for* the churches if the churches are not around during the tribulation? Verse 17 says, "The Spirit and the bride say 'Come!'" The "bride," the church on earth, longs for its union with Christ in heaven, which will last throughout all eternity. And the apostle John echoes the cry of our hearts in verse 20: "Amen. Come, Lord Jesus."

FALLACY 3:
"THE SEVEN CHURCHES REFERENCE
LITERAL ERAS OF CHURCH HISTORY"

Chapter 3

Most pretribulation rapture proponents believe that the churches in Revelation 2–3 represent literal, historical churches, as well as periods of time in church history. So Laodicea, though it was a literal ancient church, would also represent the last church era prior to the rapture. If that were the case, then why would Christ come to rescue a "lukewarm" church from the coming tribulation wrath, when he would rather vomit them out of this mouth?

Why are there multiple references to "overcoming" in the letters to the churches (Rev. 2:4, 17, 26; 3:5, 12)? Revelation 21:7 says, "He who overcomes will inherit all this, and I will be his God and he will be my son." Why the emphasis at the end of the book of Revelation on "overcoming" if there are no church saints who need to overcome?

Why do six of the seven letters to the churches contain references either to the second coming of Christ or the battle of Armageddon, if representatives from each of the churches mentioned are not all going to be around for much of the tribulation? (The letter to Smyrna is the only one without a reference to the second coming, so perhaps most people from that church have died and are with the Lord at the time of his second coming; see Rev. 13:15.)

- Revelation 2:5 addresses the church at Ephesus: "If you do not repent, I will come to you and remove your lampstand from its place."

- The Pergamum church is told to repent or "I will soon come to you and will fight against them with the sword of my mouth" (Rev. 2:16). This symbolism refers to the battle of Armageddon, where Christ uses his mouth to destroy the armies of the earth.
- To those who "overcome" from Thyatira, God says he will give the "morning star" (Rev. 2:28). The morning star represents the second coming of Christ. Incidentally, the "morning star" occurs after the "dark night," a symbol of the tribulation. (See also Rev. 22:16; 2 Peter 1:19.)
- The church of Sardis is warned to repent, or "I will come like a thief and you will not know at what time I will come to you" (Rev. 3:3). The "thief in the night" terminology is also used multiple times in the gospels in reference to the second coming of Christ. So evidently, some from Sardis will live during the tribulation and experience the second coming of Christ in a negative way.
- The church at Philadelphia is told to endure patiently so they will avoid "the hour of trial" (Rev. 3:10) that occurs after the second coming of Christ, when the subsequent bowl judgments are unleashed. The members of this church, who are around at the second coming of Christ, will be raptured out and not have to experience this tragedy.
- The church of Laodicea contains an indirect reference of the second coming of Christ: "Here I am! I stand at the door and knock. If anyone hears my voice and opens the door, I will come in and eat with him, and he with me" (Rev. 3:20). In this verse, Jesus is about to return and is "knocking" with the "signs of the times," as discussed in Luke 12:35–36: "Be dressed ready for service and keep your lamps burning, like men waiting for their master to return from a wedding banquet, so that when he comes and knocks they can immediately open the door for him." So some people in the church of Laodicea will be around to see the signs that tell them Jesus is "knocking at the door" and about to return.

Though I believe people from all seven churches will be present until the second coming of Christ, only two of these churches—Smyrna and

Philadelphia—will have positive testimonies for Christ through the tribulation. The true tribulation saints will eventually have to exit the last Babylon, leaving their respective apostate churches, and join the underground church network, represented by the church at Philadelphia, or be captured and killed as part of the church of Smyrna. Incidentally, these two positive church lights for Christ during the tribulation line up with the symbolism of the "two lampstands" and with the "two witnesses" (Rev. 11; Zech. 4).

It's also interesting that John refers to himself as his readers' "companion in tribulation" (Rev. 1:9 KJV). Likewise the churches will have to suffer persecution and trials, just as Christians have throughout history. Second Timothy 3:12 states, "everyone who wants to live a godly life in Christ Jesus will be persecuted." In John 15:20, Jesus said that if they persecuted him, they will persecute his followers. If the "church age" started off with extreme persecution of the saints, then why wouldn't we expect it to finish with severe tribulation?

Chapter 4

When discussing the timing of the rapture, pretribulation proponents are quick to quote Mark 13:32: "No one knows about that day or hour, not even the angels in heaven, nor the Son, but only the Father." They say the rapture cannot occur at the end of tribulation, because everyone would know the exact timing, based on knowing when tribulation begins. Therefore, he could not come as a thief in the night to "all." However, the Greek word translated "knows" in this verse is *eido*, which is past to present tense, meaning the original readers, as well as all previous generations, did not and could not know when the second coming of Christ will be. The future tense for "knows" was not used here because end-times believers will be capable of knowing. In fact, every time the Bible discusses knowing about the time or the day of Christ's return, it uses this Greek word *eido*. Another word for "knows"—*ginosko*—was also never used in conjunction with these verses, as this would include having complete, intimate knowledge of the future as well as the past and present.

Scripture also certainly supports the fact that many tribulation saints will not be surprised about the second coming of Christ. First Thessalonians 5:4–6 states, "But you, brothers, are not in darkness so that this day should surprise you like a thief. You are all sons of the light and sons of the day. We do not belong to the night or to the darkness. So then, let us not be like others, who are asleep, but let us be alert and self-controlled." Those who live in spiritual darkness will be surprised by Christ's second coming, but believers should not be if they know the Scriptures and have discernment. Second Thessalonians 2:1–8 discusses the events that will occur before the day of the Lord—such as the rebellion and the revealing of the Antichrist—so tribulation saints should know when to expect their Master's return.

James 5:7 says, "Be patient, then, brothers, until the Lord's coming. See how the farmer waits for the land to yield its valuable crop." Likewise we can see the signs of the times "growing," which should make the return of Christ no great surprise to his saints. Luke 21:28 sums up our expected response to the signs that occur prior to the second coming of Christ: "When these things begin to take place, stand up and lift up your heads, because your redemption is drawing near." Our redemption is completed at the second coming of Christ and rapture.

Jesus rebuked the people for their lack of understanding of the times: "When you see a cloud rising in the west, immediately you say, 'It's going to rain,' and it does. And when the south wind blows, you say, 'It's going to be hot,' and it is. Hypocrites! You know how to interpret the appearance of the earth and the sky. How is it that you don't know how to interpret this present time?" (Luke 12:54–56). So the wise end-times saints will be able to see the signs of the times, and should know the day of Jesus' coming.

Luke 12:35–39 covers the two ways Christ will return through the door of every house at the second coming. To his saints who are ready for the wedding banquet with their lamps burning, he will come knocking, and the outcome will be blissful. However, he will break in like a thief to the houses of those who don't know him, and they will suffer an unending, unimaginable nightmare! They are the ones Luke 12:40 is warning: "You also must be ready, because the Son of Man will come at an hour when you do not expect him." In Luke 12:41–46, Jesus answered the question asked by Peter, and many Christians today, about who the warning was addressed to. The servant who doesn't act as a "faithful and wise manager" is the one to whom the master will return on a "day when he does not expect and at an hour he is not aware of."

Matthew 24:37–41 describes two different outcomes for those who are alive at the second coming of Christ:

> As it was in the days of Noah, so it will be at the coming of the Son of Man. For in the days before the flood, people were eating and drinking, marrying and giving in marriage, up to the day Noah entered the ark; and they knew nothing about what would happen until the flood came and took them all away. That is how it will be at the coming of the Son of Man. Two men will be in the field; one will be taken and the other left. Two women will be grinding with a hand mill; one will be taken and the other left.

Noah knew when the wrath of God was coming, and the day he went into the ark the wrath started. Likewise, Lot was told to leave Sodom and Gomorrah shortly before it was destroyed. Amos 3:7 says, "Surely the Sovereign LORD does nothing without revealing his plan to his servants the prophets." Though we are not prophets and Jesus is the last prophet, would it not be consistent for God to reveal his plan to the tribulation saints who diligently seek him? John 16:13 says, "But when he, the Spirit of truth, comes, he will guide you into all truth, . . . and he will tell you what is yet to come."

I do believe the exact hour or moment of Christ's return will not be known until it actually occurs, because other scriptures support that: "Be on guard! Be alert! You do not know when that time will come" (Mark 13:33). But subsequent verses clarify that the "time" is the moment or hour—not the day—of his coming. So the "hour" will not be known until it occurs, but in any case, the elect should not be surprised.

> It's like a man going away: He leaves his house and puts his servants in charge, each with his assigned task, and tells the one at the door to keep watch.
>
> Therefore keep watch because you do not know when the owner of the house will come back—whether in

the evening, or at midnight, or when the rooster crows, or at dawn. If he comes suddenly, do not let him find you sleeping. What I say to you I say to everyone: "Watch!"

—Mark 13:34–37

Though other verses confirm that we will not know the *hour* of Christ's return, many scriptures show that tribulation saints can know the *day* of his return. (More about this in chapter 14.) The Spirit-led believer in Christ should not be surprised by the timing of the second coming. Many will know and will be encouraged as they anticipate the return of their Savior.

Chapter 5

Second Thessalonians 2:1–10 talks of a "restraining force" holding back the Antichrist from being revealed, which pretribulation rapture proponents believe is none other than "the church" or the Holy Spirit. Yet, nowhere in Scripture is this term used to describe the Spirit or the church. Either the Spirit is called what he is—the Spirit—or the symbolism used is a clear reference to the Spirit. The church is called the "bride of Christ" and the "body of Christ," among other equally clear terms, but never a "restraining force."

The Church or the Holy Spirit?

If God were to remove the church and the Holy Spirit at a pretribulation rapture, then not a single person would come to Christ during the tribulation, unless the Holy Spirit were to return to the earth again. But there's no mention of the restraining force being reinstated. Some may say the Holy Spirit will not be required for anyone to be saved during the tribulation, just as Old Testament saints were saved without the indwelling Spirit. My response to that is to say that God would not go backward to an earlier and inferior dispensation during the tribulation. First Peter 1:10–13 tells how the prophets and angels longed to see the fulfillment of this superior dispensation of Jesus and the Holy Spirit in us.

Before drawing any conclusions on the matter of the restraining force, let's review 2 Thessalonians 2:5–7: "Don't you remember that when I was with you I used to tell you these things? And now you know what is holding him back, so that he may be revealed at the proper time. For the secret power of lawlessness is already at work; but the one who now holds it back will continue to do so till he is taken out of the way." It seems Paul would have told the Thessalonians they were the "restraining force," if indeed he was referring to the church—the saints who would be alive at the second coming.

So if Paul was not talking about the Holy Spirit or the church, what is the restraining force that has to get "out of the way" before the Antichrist is to be fully revealed (2 Thess. 2:5–7)?

A System of Government?

Some believe the answer may be a governmental power system that must relinquish its power to the Antichrist, perhaps the revised Roman Empire, from which the Antichrist is thought to come. Revelation 17:12–13 says, "The ten horns you saw are the ten kings who have not yet received a kingdom, but who for one hour will receive authority as kings along with the beast. They have one purpose and will give their power and authority to the beast." Others think the government system is the United States, which has to get out of the way to give the authority to the Revised Roman Empire, which ultimately gives power to the Antichrist.

The Archangel Michael?

I believe the restraining force is the archangel Michael, the protector of God's people. The restraining force is referred to in 2 Thessalonians 2:5–7 as "what," "the one," and "he" all in the same cluster of verses. It appears, then, to be a single entity that is neuter form in reality, but can be referred to in the masculine for grammatical purposes. As an angel, Michael is neither male nor female, but he is often referenced in masculine terms, whereas the church is typically referred to with a feminine pronoun.

Daniel 12:1 offers more support for the archangel Michael being the restraining force: "At that time Michael, the great prince who protects your people, will arise. There will be a time of distress such as has not happened from the beginning of nations until then. But at that time your people—everyone whose name is found written in the book—will be delivered." So Michael protects the people of God, but will stand up to get out of the way to allow the Antichrist to be revealed and start the most severe persecution ever seen for Israel. Though God's people will face the incredibly hard times after the Antichrist is in control, they will be delivered through the great tribulation period, or "Jacob's trouble," with the help of God and his angelic messengers.

Some mid-tribulation rapture proponents claim the verses describing "deliverance" imply that the time Michael stands up is the very day the church is raptured. This is not true, as Daniel 12:7 clarifies the time interval of the persecution: "It will be for a time, times and half a time. When the power of the holy people has been finally broken, all these things will be completed." So for forty-two months, or three and a half years after the "abomination of desolation," God's holy people will be severely persecuted. Then, when they can take it no longer, Christ returns. Daniel 12:11 says there will be 1,290 days until the end from the Jewish perspective. (More on this in chapter 12.) Though Michael stands up, removing his restraining force on Satan at the middle of the tribulation period, he is still in the business of protecting God's people.

Chapter 6

FALLACY 6:
"THE SEVENTH TRUMPET AND
THE LAST TRUMPET CALL OF
GOD OCCUR IN TWO DISTINCT
CONTEXTS"

M any pretribulation rapture proponents claim the last trumpet call of God occurs at the rapture (1 Thess. 4:16), and the seventh trumpet that is sounded by an angel (Rev. 10:7; 11:15–18) occurs at a much later time within the tribulation period. Because the last trumpet signals the rapture, however, a pretribulation-rapture position would have the seven trumpets sounding after the "last" trumpet (of God), which, frankly, makes no sense at all.

A closer examination of the passages that talk about the seventh trumpet and the trumpet call of God shows that both refer to the same series of events—cataclysmic signs on earth and in the heavens, the church raptured, and the final tribulation wrath of God beginning. So we would have complete harmony in Scripture on the issue of the last trumpet if the angel were to sound the seventh trumpet first and then God were to immediately sound the last trumpet of the tribulation, with both occurring in the same context.

The verses dealing with the second coming reference a common description of a trumpet call. This commonality also supports the view that the second coming and rapture occur together. For example,

- "Blow the trumpet in Zion; sound the alarm on my holy hill. Let all who live in the land tremble, for the day of the LORD is coming. It is close at hand—a day of darkness and gloom, a day of clouds and blackness" (Joel 2:1–2).

- "The great day of the LORD is near—near and coming quickly. Listen! The cry on the day of the LORD will be bitter, the shouting of the warrior there. That day will be a day of wrath, a day of distress and anguish, a day of trouble and ruin, a day of darkness and gloom, a day of clouds and blackness, a day of trumpet and battle cry against the fortified cities and against the corner towers" (Zeph. 1:14–16).
- "Then the LORD will appear over them; his arrow will flash like lightning. The Sovereign LORD will sound the trumpet" (Zech. 9:14).
- "And he will send his angels with a loud trumpet call, and they will gather his elect from the four winds, from one end of the heavens to another" (Matt. 24:31).
- "For the Lord himself will come down from heaven, with a loud command, with the voice of the archangel and the trumpet call of God, and the dead in Christ will rise first. After that, we who are still alive and are left will be caught up together with them in the clouds to meet the Lord in the air" (1 Thess. 4:16–17).
- "Listen, I tell you a mystery: We will not all sleep, but we will all be changed—in a flash, in the twinkling of an eye, at the last trumpet. For the trumpet will sound, the dead will be raised imperishable, and we will be changed" (1 Cor. 15:51–52).
- "But in the days when the seventh angel is about to sound his trumpet, the mystery of God will be accomplished" (Rev. 10:7).

Last, in Revelation 11:15, the seventh trumpet sounds, and the raptured saints in heaven talk about the coming millennial kingdom and praise God. Then in verse 18, the twenty-four elders say, "The time has come for judging the dead, and for rewarding your servants the prophets and your saints and those who reverence your name, both small and great—and for destroying those who destroy the earth." The judgment for the righteous is generally accepted to occur immediately after the rapture. And the time for "destroying" refers to that final "hour of testing" that occurs for the people left on the earth after the rapture and second coming.

After the battle of Armageddon, and after the end of the tribulation, another distinctly different trumpet call signals the ingathering of the dispersed Jews and Gentiles to Mount Zion in preparation for the start of the millennial kingdom (Isa. 27:12–13). There are other trumpets sounded throughout the time of the millennial kingdom, but there is only one "last trumpet" of the tribulation.

Chapter 7

Discussion on the "end of the age of the Gentiles" gives support for the church being present throughout most of the tribulation. The age of the Gentiles started at Pentecost, after the Jews rejected Christ at his first coming, and it will conclude when the church is raptured. Romans 11:25–27 discusses how "Israel has experienced a hardening in part until the full number of the Gentiles has come in." That number is complete at the rapture.

In Luke 21, Jesus is discussing the setting of the "end of the ages." Verses 23–24 read, "How dreadful it will be in those days for pregnant women and nursing mothers! There will be great distress in the land and wrath against this people. They will fall by the sword and will be taken prisoners to all the nations. Jerusalem will be trampled on by the Gentiles until the times of the Gentiles are fulfilled." Then in verses 27–28 Jesus describes his second coming and the rapture of the church: "At that time they will see the Son of Man coming in a cloud with power and great glory. When these things begin to take place, stand up and lift up your heads, because your redemption is drawing near." From these verses, we can see that the age of the Gentiles will last up until the second coming.

Many pretribulation advocates believe that the trampling by Gentiles has ended since Israel became a nation again in 1948 and that the stage is now set for the pretribulation rapture. But take a look at Revelation 11:1–3, where reference is made to the rebuilding of the Jewish temple during the beginning of tribulation. After the Antichrist gets ultimate power at the midpoint of tribulation, he defiles the temple, an act called the "abomination of desolation," when all worship of God will stop and verse 2 will then take place: "They will trample on the holy city for 42 months." So the age of the Gentiles will last for three-and-a-half years, until the second coming of Christ and rapture of the church.

Chapter 8

Another support for the rapture occurring at the second coming revolves around the discussion of the first and second resurrections mentioned in Revelation 20:4d–6:

> They came to life and reigned with Christ a thousand years. (The rest of the dead did not come to life until the thousand years were ended.) This is the first resurrection. Blessed and holy are those that have part in the first resurrection. The second death has no power over them, but they will be priests of God and of Christ and will reign with him for a thousand years.

The first resurrection occurs at the rapture. We who are raptured will all later reign with Christ and judge the world through the millennium. At the first resurrection the bodies of those who died prior to the rapture are raised and glorified as they meet their spirits from heaven. (See also 1 Cor. 15:51–54.) The second resurrection is for unbelievers. So there are clearly two distinct general resurrections of the bodies of the dead: one for the saved in Christ at the rapture of the church, and one for the unsaved at the end of the millennium. (Yes, there is an exception to the first resurrection [the rapture]: Jesus Christ, who was the very first resurrection.)

If we were to postulate a pretribulation rapture, then there could not be just one general first resurrection. Certainly, some of the new converts to Christ during the tribulation will be martyred for their faith. They would have missed the rapture, failed to get a resurrected body, and thus would not be privileged to serve in the millennial kingdom as judges for Christ. The only way around this dilemma would be for those saints who were martyred during the tribulation to have individual resurrections, meaning multiple raptures, after the pretribulation rapture; but there is no scriptural support for this. The rapture at the second coming—a single, general rapture—would not create this dilemma.

Another dilemma for pretribulation rapture proponents is the reference in Revelation 20:4 to raptured saints reigning with Christ for 1,000 years before the second resurrection. A pretribulation rapture would require them to "come to life" seven years before the millennial kingdom 1,007 years until the end of the millennial kingdom, instead of 1,000 years, that is clearly mentioned here. Scriptures clearly do not support the raptured saints waiting in heaven seven years before reigning in the millennial kingdom.

Clarifying Other Resurrection References

Some pretribulation rapture advocates may refer to Matthew 27:52 to suggest that a "first resurrection" is not a generalized single event. This verse talks about dead saints coming out of their tombs on the day of Jesus' crucifixion, "and after Jesus' resurrection they went into the holy city and appeared to many people." These individuals did not have glorified bodies; they were just revived corpses. Heaven was not opened up until Jesus rose on the third day, so these bodies could not have been glorified or resurrected before Jesus was. If these were glorified bodies, they would have preceded Jesus' resurrection, which would be a contradiction of the Scriptures. This reference points to the eventual general first resurrection, when Christ returns. It also symbolizes the victory Christ Jesus has given us over death, that something miraculous occurred both physically and spiritually at his crucifixion.

A few other verses seem to indicate that the first and second resurrections might occur simultaneously, but we know from the discussion in Revelation 20 that the events are separated by a thousand years. First, Daniel 12:2 says, "Multitudes who sleep in the dust of the earth will awake: some to everlasting life, others to shame and everlasting contempt." Then, John 5:28–29 states, "Do not be amazed at this, for a time is coming when all who are in their graves will hear his voice and come out—those who have done good will rise to live, and those who have done evil will rise to be condemned." These verses are an example of prophecies being "telescoped." They speak of events that, though they're separated by many years, because of their similarities, are discussed in the same verse or verses. The pretribulation rapture proponents would say, "You have just validated why we say all the verses on the second coming and rapture appear to place the two events together, but indeed they are separated by at least seven years." I respond by saying there are so many detailed verses on the end times that are not telescoped (e.g., Rev. 22:4b) and give complete clarity to the timing of events that this cannot be possible without contradicting Scripture.

PART 2
TIMING IS EVERYTHING IN
CLEARING THE DECEPTION

B efore we look at the many references to the rapture, let's expand our understanding of the second coming of Christ, which occurs when the sixth seal is opened. Revelation 6:12–17 talks about the sixth seal being the time of God's wrath: the sun turns black, the moon turns to blood, the stars fall from the sky, and every mountain and island is removed from its place. In verse 16 the people are asking for the rocks to fall down on them and kill them to hide them from "the face of him who sits on the throne"—none other than Jesus Christ, who is literally on top of Mount Zion, displaying some of his glory for the whole world to see; but to the unsaved of humanity it will be a dreadful sight for his light to shine on all their sin. So the sixth seal is clearly associated with the second coming and the cataclysmic events associated with his return.

To give further support that the sixth seal is indeed the second coming, let us briefly digress to some parallel Old Testament passages that refer to the second coming of Christ, and use terminology and symbolism similar to the New Testament description of the sixth seal.

- "The sun will be turned to darkness and the moon to blood before the coming of the great and dreadful day of the LORD. And everyone who calls on the name of the LORD will be saved; for on Mount Zion and in Jerusalem there will be deliverance, as the LORD has said, among the survivors whom the LORD calls"

(Joel 2:31–32). In his sermon on the Day of Pentecost, Peter quotes this passage from Joel (Acts 2:16–21).

- "Men will flee to caves in the rocks" (Isa. 2:19).
- "All the starry host will fall like withered leaves from the vine, like shriveled figs from the fig tree" (Isa. 34:4).
- "Who can endure the day of his coming? Who can stand when he appears?" (Mal. 3:2).
- "The mountains quake before him and the hills melt away. The earth trembles at his presence, the world and all who live in it. Who can withstand his indignation?" (Nah. 1:5–6).
- "You alone are to be feared. Who can stand before you when you are angry?" (Ps. 76:7).

Revelation 10

Verses 1–3

In Revelation 10, we see that the rapture occurs at the seventh trumpet judgment, which happens in the same setting as the second coming. So the seventh trumpet judgment occurs in the same context as the sixth seal. Discussion in Revelation 10:1–3a, references the second coming of Christ:

> Then I saw another mighty angel coming down from heaven. He was robed in a cloud with a rainbow above his head; his face was like the sun, and his legs were like fiery pillars. He was holding a little scroll, which lay open in his hand. He planted his right foot on the sea and his left foot on the land, and he gave a loud shout like the roar of a lion.

The angel in this passage is Jesus Christ—although he's no ordinary angel. (See also Gen. 16:1–22:19; Ex. 23:20; Num. 22:23; Ps. 34:7; and see Ezek. 1:25–28 for a similar description of God or Christ as an angel.) The "fiery pillars" are the legs of Christ, also mentioned as being made of bronze in Revelation 1:15 and in Zechariah 6:1, symbolizing judgment. The feet of this angel are standing "on the sea" and "on the land" to symbolize that Christ's judgments at his second coming will affect the whole earth. There is one difference between the position of Jesus as he is standing at the seventh trumpet but is sitting at the sixth seal. It appears that Jesus is sitting on the throne as he appears in the sky at the second coming, however, once he arrives at Mount Zion He stands; all these events occur in the same setting. (See Matt. 25:31; Zech. 14:1–5.)

Verse 6

In verse 6 (KJV), Christ makes a unique statement: "Time is no longer!" The NIV renders it "There will be no more delay!" But we know from Habakkuk 2:3 and other references that God may linger, but he "does not delay." The truest interpretation here is that time will end for raptured saints, who will be in the "eternal state," where time is no longer. Those "left behind" will experience the last day of life on the earth as they know it—the stars will vanish from the sky, and the sun and moon will stand still. The glory of the Lord will fill the earth, and this age will end. (See Hab. 3:11; Isa. 34:4; 40:4; Joel 2:30–31.) The sun and moon stand still (Hab. 3:11), I believe, until the end of the tribulation. With the rotation of the earth stopped, men will indeed be in "anguish and perplexity at the roaring and tossing of the sea" (Luke 21:25–26).

So, the seventh trumpet is no ordinary event, but is associated with the rapture of the church in conjunction with the second coming of Christ at the "end of time" for this age.

Verse 7

"But in the days when the seventh angel is about to sound his trumpet, the mystery of God will be accomplished, just as he announced to his servants the prophets" (Rev. 10:7). The "mystery of God" is multifaceted but will include the completed understanding of all God's revelation that can be known. No revelation of the gospel is completely understood until we are with God, as Paul wrote in 1 Corinthians 13:12: "Now we see but a poor reflection as in a mirror; then we shall see face to face. Now I know in part; then I shall know fully, even as I am fully known." One aspect to the "mystery" is the rapture: "Listen, I tell you a mystery: We will not all sleep, but we will all be changed—in a flash, in the twinkling of an eye, at the last trumpet" (1 Cor. 15:51–52). The rapture will be an instantaneous glorification at the last trumpet, and we'll completely understand its mystery, once we experience it.

There are several other mysteries referenced in the Bible. The mystery of the union of Christ and the church (Eph. 5:32) will be understood at the rapture. The mystery of the gospel (Eph. 6:19) and its impact on the world will be fully realized at the rapture. The mystery of "Christ in you" (Col. 1:27) and the "mystery of godliness" (1 Tim. 3:16) will be revealed when our bodies are resurrected and emanate the glory of Christ for all to see. The "mystery of God, namely Christ" (Col. 2:2), will be completed for us at the rapture, so we'll have a clearer understanding of the Trinity at this point. Romans 11:25 states, "I do not want you to be ignorant of this mystery, brothers, so that you may not be conceited: Israel has experienced a hardening in part until the full number of the Gentiles has come in." The mystery of the Gentiles coming in is completed at the rapture and the end of the age of the Gentiles. Habakkuk 2:3 says, "For the revelation awaits an appointed time; it speaks of the end." The end of time occurs at the rapture, our time of complete revelation.

Verses 8–11

After the seventh trumpet is sounded and the mystery is revealed, we see one more reference, albeit symbolic to the rapture in chapter 10:

> Then the voice that I had heard from heaven spoke to me once more: "Go, take the scroll that lies open in the hand of the angel who is standing on the sea and on the land."
>
> So I went to the angel and asked him to give me the little scroll. He said to me, "Take it and eat it. It will turn your stomach sour, but in your mouth it will be as sweet as honey." I took the little scroll from the angel's hand and ate it. It tasted as sweet as honey in my mouth, but when I had eaten it, my stomach turned

sour. Then I was told, "You must prophesy again about
many peoples, nations, languages and kings."

—Rev. 10:8–11

The reason the scroll tasted sweet in John's mouth is that it is symbolic for the rapture and Jesus reigning in righteousness over the world. The souring of John's stomach is identified with the awful wrath of God upon the earth that lasts from the second coming until the end of the tribulation. (See also Ezek. 2:9–3:3.)

Incidentally, the "little scroll" of Revelation 10 is a prophetic detailing of end-times events and should not be confused with the scroll mentioned in Revelation 5, which represents the "title deed for the earth." This title-deed scroll has "writing on both sides" and "seven seals" that only the Lamb can open (Rev. 5:1, 5). This scroll will not be swallowed and will not be opened completely until after the second coming and rapture. Its seventh seal, broken after the second coming, will usher in the judgment of the saints, followed by the "hour of testing" associated with the bowl judgments. Prior to Christ's second coming, Satan is prince of the earth (Eph. 2:2), but once the title deed's prophecy is fulfilled, Christ will become the final and ultimate Prince of the earth.

Revelation 11

Verse 15

The next reference to the rapture is found in Revelation 11:15: "The seventh angel sounded his trumpet, and there were loud voices in heaven, which said: 'The kingdom of the world has become the kingdom of our Lord and of his Christ, and he will reign for ever and ever.'" Clearly the rapture occurs in context with the seventh trumpet judgment, so how could this statement be true with a pretribulation rapture? In that case God's kingdom would have to start during the tribulation period. But we know that this is when Satan's kingdom is being magnified on planet earth. God's kingdom does not begin until seven years later, when he arrives at the second coming near the end of tribulation.

Verse 18

The tribulation wrath of God arrives at the seventh trumpet: "The nations were angry; and your wrath has come. The time has come for judging the dead and for rewarding your servants the prophets and your saints and those who reverence your name, both small and great—and for destroying those who destroy the earth" (Rev. 11:18). Notice that the second coming of Christ has two aspects: the grace of God shown to his elect, and the wrath of God shown to the ungodly. The spirits (or souls) of those who have died—including those from Old Testament times to the present—prior to the rapture are with God in heaven at this point, but they don't get glorified bodies and are not judged until the rapture.

Revelation 14

The raptured 144,000 Jewish evangelists are discussed in Revelation 14:1–5. Verses 14–16 refer to the rapture as the "harvest of the earth."

Revelation 15

Verses 1–2

Revelation 15:1–2 contains a more subtle reference to the raptured saints:

> I saw in heaven another great and marvelous sign: seven angels with the seven last plagues—last, because with them God's wrath is completed. And I saw what looked like a sea of glass mixed with fire and, standing beside the sea, those who had been victorious over the beast and his image and over the number of his name. They held harps given them by God and sang the song of Moses the servant of God and the song of the Lamb.

The "sea of glass mixed with fire" is the earth being judged by the wrath of God, but the raptured saints are "standing beside the sea," and are observing the bowl judgments that occur after the rapture. (See also 2 Peter 3:10; Joel 2:3–11; Rev. 8:5; 16:8.)

Verse 8

Revelation 15:8 states, "And the temple was filled with smoke from the glory of God and from his power, and no one could enter the temple until the seven plagues (the seven bowl judgments) of the seven angels were completed." It appears, then, that God is so solemn about what is to transpire with the bowl judgments that he wants to be left alone. Ezekiel 33:11 reminds us that God takes "no pleasure in the death of the wicked." Even though the raptured saints may be separated from God at this time, we will still be with Jesus. In the "eternal state" there are at least two distinct manifestations of the Trinity: "the Lamb" and the "Lord God Almighty" (Rev. 21:22). We must remember that the judging is left to Jesus, as John 5:22 states: "Moreover, the Father judges no one, but has entrusted all judgment to the Son."

Revelation 19

Notice that the next mention of the raptured saints in Revelation describes them as the "great multitude" (Rev. 19:1) praising God while they watch the bowl judgments unleashed upon the earth. They even use the word *hallelujah* multiple times. Notice that this is hardly a time of great silence in heaven, because the judgment of the righteous is over, and finally God's judgment will be completed on the earth.

Chapter 10

THE WEDDING SUPPER OF THE
LAMB

W e touched on the wedding supper of the Lamb in chapter 2, but now let us look in more detail at the timing of the wedding supper of the Lamb to see if it gives support for the timing of the rapture. In first-century Israel, as in twenty-first-century America, a wedding banquet typically started shortly after the wedding concluded. It would make no sense to have a party to celebrate the wedding seven years after the event—when the bride and groom have a mortgage, two children, and a golden retriever. So it makes no logical sense for the rapture to occur prior to the tribulation. The wedding supper of the Lamb is a celebration of the Bridegroom (Jesus Christ) and the bride (the church) finally being joined together for all eternity. The wedding occurs shortly after the rapture of the church when the bride and groom are united, after the church is glorified and the saints are subsequently judged.

The Parable of the Wedding Banquet

Matthew 22:1–14 relates the parable of the wedding banquet, in which a king (God) prepared a banquet for his son (Jesus). "He sent his servants to those who had been invited to the banquet to tell them to come, but they refused to come" (Matt. 22:3). Not only did they refuse, they "seized his servants, mistreated them and killed them" (Matt. 22:6). "The king was enraged" and "said to his servants, 'The wedding banquet is ready, but those I invited did not deserve to come. Go to the street corners and invite to the banquet anyone you find'" (Matt. 22:8–9). Through this parable, Jesus was telling his Jewish listeners that since they and their ancestors had rejected God's word spoken through the prophets, the good news of the gospel was being offered to the Gentiles.

Verse 11 then says "the king . . . noticed a man there who was not wearing wedding clothes." When the king asked how the man had gotten in without proper attire, the man had no answer. As a result, he was thrown "outside, into the darkness, where there will be weeping and gnashing of teeth" (Matt. 22:13). The place of "weeping and gnashing of teeth" is often referred to as *gehenna*, the lake of fire. This unfortunate individual was invited, but the Holy Spirit had not changed his life, as he was not truly saved and definitely not "chosen."

Other "Feasting" References

Luke 13:24–29 (and see Matt. 8:11–12) discusses a "feast in the kingdom of God," and verse 25 notes, "Once the owner of the house gets up and closes the door, you will stand outside knocking and pleading." This occurs when Christ gets up to return for the second coming and closes the door of the kingdom of God on the unsaved. Verses 28–29 say,

> There will be weeping there, and gnashing of teeth, when you see Abraham, Isaac and Jacob and all the prophets in the kingdom of God, but you yourselves thrown out. People will come from east and west and north and south, and will take their places at the feast in the kingdom of God.

In this passage, the feasting again includes the raptured saints, but this time it also includes the believers from the millennium period. (See also Zech. 14:16–19; Isa. 49:12; 55:1; 59:19.) Notice that the raptured saints are visualized by the unsaved of humanity.

Later in Luke, Jesus encouraged believers to give banquets for the poor because "you will be repaid at the resurrection of the righteous" (Luke 14:12–14). This again implies a great banquet in heaven for the saints shortly after the rapture.

Gehenna

References to gehenna in the parables give us further clues to the timing of the rapture and the subsequent wedding feast. Gehenna is not used as a place of judgment until, near the end of the tribulation, the Beast and False Prophet are thrown into the lake of fire after their defeat in the battle of Armageddon. (See Rev. 19:19–21.)

Matthew 25:31–46 talks about the "sorting process" that takes place at the end of the tribulation. At this time all survivors of the tribulation are brought before the Lord. True believers are allowed to enter the millennial kingdom, but those who rejected Christ will be thrown to gehenna. So the Beast and the False Prophet get some company in the fiery lake at the end of the tribulation.

Now, if we take Jesus' descriptions in the banquet parables literally— "darkness," "weeping and gnashing of teeth," and so forth—then a pretribulation rapture would contradict the Scriptures, since gehenna is not used as a place of torment until at least after the battle of Armageddon. All the unsaved who die prior to the end of the tribulation, except the Beast and False Prophet, will go to hades initially, and will not go to gehenna until after the "great white throne judgment" at the end of the millennial kingdom. (See Rev. 20:11–15.) So for a pretribulation rapture to be true, those dying without Christ during the tribulation would have to go to gehenna, which would mean they would precede the Beast and False Prophet, since these two don't go to gehenna until they are defeated in the battle of Armageddon. If this parable is true in its more literal application, then a pretribulation rapture is impossible.

Chapter 11

I dentifying the sequencing of the battle of Armageddon in Scripture will help us to further appreciate the timing of the rapture and second coming. Let's take a look at several passages.

Revelation 14

Revelation 14 gives us a glimpse of the horror of the last battle of this age:

> Another angel came out of the temple in heaven, and he too had a sharp sickle. . . . The angel swung his sickle on the earth, gathered its grapes and threw them into the great winepress of God's wrath. They were trampled in the winepress outside the city and blood flowed out of the press, rising as high as the horses' bridles for a distance of 1,600 stadia.
>
> —Rev. 14:17, 19–20

This final bloodbath covers about 160 miles, a veritable sea of blood about four feet deep.

Revelation 16

The Sixth Bowl

The sixth bowl judgment is what actually sets up the battle of Armageddon. Revelation 16:12–16 says the "great river Euphrates" will dry up to allow the "kings from the East" to come against Israel at a place "called Armageddon." Of course, getting several world leaders together in one place is no small task, especially when considering the "earth dwellers" will be trying to hide in rocks from the fear of the Lamb at the sixth seal or second coming. In this case, it takes a trio of demons.

> Then I saw three evil spirits that looked like frogs; they came out of the mouth of the dragon, out of the mouth of the beast and out of the mouth of the false prophet. They are spirits of demons performing miraculous signs, and they go out to the kings of the whole world, to gather them for the battle on the great day of God Almighty.
>
> —Rev. 16:13–14

The Seventh Bowl

With the seventh bowl judgment the actual battle of Armageddon occurs.

> Then they gathered the kings together to the place that in Hebrew is called Armageddon. The seventh angel poured out his bowl into the air, and out of the temple came a loud voice from the throne, saying, "It is done!" Then there came flashes of lightning, rumblings, peals of thunder and a severe earthquake. No earthquake like it has ever occurred since man has been on earth, so tremendous was the quake. The great city split into three parts, and the cities of the nations collapsed. God remembered Babylon the Great and gave her the cup filled with the wine of the fury of his wrath. Every island

fled away and the mountains could not be found. From the sky huge hailstones of about a hundred pounds each fell upon men. And they cursed God on account of the plague of hail, because the plague was so terrible.

—Rev. 16:16–21

Other Significant "Armageddon" Passages

New Testament

Matthew 24:27–28 says, "For as lightning that comes from the east is visible even in the west, so will be the coming of the Son of Man. Where there is a carcass there the vultures will gather." The vultures will gather to eat the dead bodies after the battle of Armageddon, which appears to occur shortly after the second coming of Christ.

Revelation 19:6–8 describes the raptured "great multitude" in heaven and the "bride" of Christ, and then verses 11–19 show Christ with the heavenly armies fighting the Beast at the battle of Armageddon. So, again, it appears the battle occurs shortly after the second coming.

Old Testament

In Zechariah 14:1–4 we read,

> A day of the LORD is coming when your plunder will be divided among you.

> I will gather all the nations to Jerusalem to fight against it; the city will be captured, the houses ransacked, and the women raped. Half of the city will go into exile, but the rest of the people will not be taken from the city.

> Then the LORD will go out and fight against those nations, as he fights in the day of battle. On that day his feet will stand on the Mount of Olives.

In this passage, the second coming of Christ takes place at a time when forces are invading Jerusalem. This, however, is not the actual battle of Armageddon. We know this because verse 12 mentions a "plague" inflicted against the nations that attack Jerusalem and not a "winepress." (See Rev. 14:19–20.) We will discuss this further in the chapter on Israel in prophecy, but it does appear that Jesus rescues Israel after an invasion near the end, and the battle of Armageddon follows shortly thereafter, when these forces retreat from the initial second-coming wrath.

Ezekiel 38:1–15 describes an initial invasion of Israel by "Gog" and "Magog" that may be similar to the invasion cited in Zechariah 14. Ezekiel 38:16 says, "You will advance against my people Israel like a cloud that covers the land. In days to come, O Gog, I will bring you against my land, so that the nations may know me when I show myself holy through you before their eyes." So it appears the second coming of Christ occurs shortly after this invasion, and the raptured church is what is glorified and shown before the "nations."

The next paragraph, verses 18–23, details what is likely the battle of Armageddon, which shortly follows the initial invasion:

> This is what will happen in that day: When Gog attacks the land of Israel, my hot anger will be aroused, declares the Sovereign LORD. In my zeal and fiery wrath I declare that at that time there shall be a great earthquake in the land of Israel. The fish of the sea, the birds of the air, the beasts of the field, every creature that moves along the ground, and all the people on the face of the earth will tremble at my presence. The mountains will be overturned, the cliffs will crumble and every wall will fall to the ground. I will summon a sword against Gog on all my mountains, declares the Sovereign LORD. Every man's sword will be against his brother. I will execute judgment upon him with plague and bloodshed; I will pour down torrents of rain, hailstones and burning sulfur on him and on his troops and on the many nations with him. And so I will show my greatness and my holiness, and I will make myself known in the sight of many nations. Then they will know that I am the LORD. . . . On the mountains

of Israel you will fall, you and all your troops and the nations with you. I will give you as food to all kinds of carrion birds and to the wild animals.

—Ezek. 38:18–23; 39:4

In Revelation 14:14–16 the rapture is described in symbolic terms as the time of the "harvest of the earth," which immediately precedes discussion on the "great winepress." This suggests that the battle of Armageddon occurs sometime after the rapture.

So the seventh bowl judgment is the "grand finale" of God's wrath upon the earth. It starts with the battle of Armageddon and involves the culmination of the "hour of testing." But, because of his great mercy, we, his children, will not have to experience this horrific final outpouring of God's wrath associated with the bowl judgments. Praise his name!

THE TRIBULATION THIRTY-DAY TIME DISCREPANCY CLEARLY SOLVED

Chapter 12

I n the prophetic books of Daniel and Revelation, there appears to be a discrepancy regarding the length of time that remains from the "abomination of desolation" to the end of the tribulation. Daniel 12:11 says "1,290 days," and Revelation 11:2–3 and 12:6 say "1,260 days" or 42 months. Is the Bible contradicting itself? How did we lose a month between the Old and New Testaments?

Fortunately, the same books that seem at odds also give us the answer to this conundrum. Remember, Daniel presents end-times prophecies from a Jewish, "pre-Christ" perspective, but Revelation gives the end times from a Gentile "post-Christ" perspective. Let's look at the Scriptures to find the "lost" thirty days.

Finding the "Lost" Thirty Days of the Tribulation

Before we get into the specifics of the end-times interpretation of Daniel 12, it's important to note that this passage is a telescoping prophecy. Though it deals with Antiochus Epiphanes defiling the temple (B.C. 168) and the subsequent cleansing of the temple by Judas Maccabeus (B.C. 164), this prophecy will not be completely fulfilled until the end times unfold.

In Daniel 12:11 we read, "From the time that the daily sacrifice is abolished and the abomination that causes desolation is set up, there will be 1,290 days." In other words, 1,290 days will elapse from the middle of the tribulation—when the Antichrist defiles the temple—to

§ 59

the end of Jewish church history for this age. With the exception of the 144,000 Jewish evangelists who convert to Christ near the beginning of the tribulation, "Israel has experienced a hardening in part until the full number of the Gentiles has come in" (Rom. 11:25). Since the large-scale Jewish revival does not occur until after the second coming, the Jewish timeline extends thirty days beyond the rapture, which occurs on day 1,260, coming to completion at day 1,290, which is the very end of the tribulation. Again, remember Daniel wrote to a Jewish audience before the time of Christ, while John's focus was on Gentile Christians who were awaiting Christ's return.

Interestingly, the thirty-day period fits nicely into the time frame required from the rapture to the end of the age. It starts with the "half hour of silence" in heaven (see Rev. 8:1), which lasts just over one literal week. (Remember, the "half hour" is on the prophetic time scale where one day is equivalent to one year.) Silence in Scripture is symbolic for judgment, and it appears the earth will also be silent before him at his coming. (See Zeph. 1:7; Hab. 2:20; Zech. 2:13; Amos 8:3; Ps. 76:8–9.) The judgment of the saints would likely be the reason for the silence. When we look at 1 Corinthians 3:12–15, which describes our works being tested with fire, we can better appreciate the reason for silence. It should also be appreciated that silence in heaven is a major event, since it would be impossible to do anything but shout out in praise before the King of Kings, unless mandated by God and in association with the judgment, where the focus is what we did for Christ.

The "hour of testing" is the next big event that occurs within the thirty-day period. It corresponds to the seven bowl judgments and would require just over two literal weeks. Then add five days for the end-times revival that occurs when the message of Christ is preached to those who have survived the tribulation wrath of God. It looks something like this:

Half-hour of silence	8 1/3 days
Hour of testing	16 2/3 days
Revival	5 days
Total	30 days

So, the thirty days were really only "lost" from a certain perspective. Looking at the end times with both Daniel and Revelation in mind, we can see a clear and straightforward explanation—though not everyone would agree with it.

Pretribulation Arguments

Pretribulation rapture proponents will often say the reason for the difference between 1,290 days in Daniel and 1,260 days in Revelation is that the Jewish year is shorter than the Gentile year. They offer drawn-out calculations to rationalize their view and claim the two books actually refer to the same period of time. I don't dispute the fact that the Jewish year is shorter than the Gentile year, but certainly a Jewish day is not shorter than a Gentile day. A day is what it is: twenty-four hours! God clearly says the Gentile church timeline ends 1,260 days after the abomination, and the Jewish timeline ends 1,290 days thereafter. Yes, the total tribulation period is not symmetric, in that the last half is thirty days longer than the first half, but this asymmetrical paradigm is not a contradiction of Scripture.

Another question pretribulation rapture proponents raise is this: Why does Revelation 11 say Israel will be protected in the desert from the Antichrist for 1,260 days, instead of 1,290 days, if the Jewish nation will be around for the entire 1,290 days?

Once Christ steps on Mount Zion at the 1,260 day mark, the "hour of testing" will begin. The enemies of God will be so busy evading his judgments upon the earth that they will have no time or energy to pursue the Jews in Bozrah—until there is a temporary pause in the wrath of God, allowing the enemy to gather troops against God and the raptured saints on Mount Zion for the battle of Armageddon. At that point, God and the raptured saints will be the focus of Satan's efforts and not the Jews in Bozrah. (See Rev. 19:17–21; Ps. 2:2.)

Matthew 24:22

Another probable reference to this thirty-day period can be found in Matthew 24:22: "If those days had not been cut short, no one would survive, but for the sake of the elect those days will be shortened."

(See also Luke 21:35–36.) If the rapture were to occur before the tribulation begins, then there would be no need to shorten the days the church would experience in the tribulation, because they would not be in the tribulation anyway. So these verses support the church being in the tribulation, but not for the entire time. The church will be raptured thirty days prior to the end of the tribulation and will be spared the most severe outpouring of God's tribulation wrath.

Daniel 8

Daniel 8:13–14 mentions a specific number of days from the start of sacrifice in the Jewish temple—which will be rebuilt starting in the early part of the tribulation—until the end of the defilement by the Gentiles at the second coming of Christ.

> Then I heard a holy one speaking, and another holy one said to him, "How long will it take for the vision to be fulfilled—the vision concerning the daily sacrifice, the rebellion that causes desolation, and the surrender of the sanctuary and of the host that will be trampled underfoot?"
>
> He said to me, "It will take 2,300 evenings and mornings; then the sanctuary will be reconsecrated."

The Jewish temple may take one to two years to build completely, but history shows us that the sacrifice starts at the beginning of the building stage. So once the cornerstone is laid and sacrifice is reinstituted, it will take 2,300 days (about six-and-a-half years) before the temple is reconsecrated. The temple is reconsecrated when Christ returns, which marks the end of the age of the Gentiles. (See Rev. 11:2; Luke 21:24.) The specific mention of "evenings and mornings" makes it explicit that God is talking about literal twenty-four-hour periods of time and not years, as some believe. This also correlates with the prophecy of the 1,260 and 1,290 days from mid-tribulation to the second coming and later culmination of the age for the Gentile and Jewish contingents of the church. Therefore, the sacrifice in the temple will start at day 220 from the start of the tribulation, and the saints will have encouragement knowing that they have a finite and predictable time to hope for and look forward to the second coming. When the tribulation saints see that this prophecy and the prophecy of 1,260 days are in perfect agreement, pinpointing the very day of Christ's return, their faith will be tremendously increased. They will have affirmation that Bible prophecy is true in every explicit detail and that their suffering is finite and limited.

Daniel 8:26 concludes: "The vision of the evenings and mornings that has been given you is true, but seal up the vision, for it concerns the distant future." The actual day of Christ's return will not be known until the tribulation begins, and it is then that the seal will be more completely opened, and the saints will be given encouragement and hope to look beyond their awful present circumstances toward the anticipated day of the glorious return of their Lord and Savior, Jesus Christ! What a day of worship and celebration that will be, knowing that the Master is returning this day!

Chapter 13

While we typically look to the prophetic books of Daniel and Revelation for insight into the end times, the rest of the Bible has much to say on the subject. Let's start with Psalms.

Psalm 2

Psalm 2:2, 5–6, 8 says,

> The kings of the earth take their stand and the rulers gather together against the LORD and against his Anointed One. . . . Then he rebukes them in his anger and terrifies them in his wrath, saying, "I have installed my King on Zion, my holy hill." . . . "Ask of me, and I will make the nations your inheritance."

Here the kings of the earth see the Lord at Mount Zion at his second coming, and they rise up against him at the battle of Armageddon. Ultimately, he wins and establishes his millennial kingdom.

Psalm 11

In Psalm 11:3–7 we read,

> When the foundations are being destroyed, what can the righteous do? The LORD is in his holy temple; the LORD is on his heavenly throne. He observes

the sons of men; his eyes examine them. The LORD examines the righteous, but the wicked and those who love violence his soul hates. On the wicked he will rain fiery coals and burning sulfur; a scorching wind will be their lot. For the LORD is righteous, he loves justice; upright men will see his face.

The ultimate fulfillment of this prophecy will occur as the foundations of the earth are being destroyed at the second coming, but the righteous believers will be protected because they have been raptured and will see the Lord and be examined in the judgment of the saints.

Psalm 14

In Psalm 14:2–3 David wrote about a unique time in history—after the rapture—when there will be no human witness for Christ on earth: "The LORD looks down from heaven on the sons of men to see if there are any who understand, any who seek God. All have turned aside, they have together become corrupt; there is no one who does good, not even one."

After the rapture and second coming, a remnant of Jews will eventually convert to Christ. There will also be a "last days" Gentile revival, but at this time there is literally no righteous believing saint in all the earth. The only testimonies for Christ during this time come from three angels who proclaim the gospel and judgment to the world. (See Rev. 14:6–11.)

Verses 5 and 7 then say, "There they are, overwhelmed with dread, for God is present in the company of the righteous. . . . Oh, that salvation for Israel would come out of Zion! When the LORD restores the fortunes of his people, let Jacob rejoice and Israel be glad!" Notice that at the second coming, described in verse 5, the ungodly will see God and the righteous saints raptured on Mount Zion. Then, in verse 7, there is pleading for the restoration of Israel that will occur near the end of the tribulation, when the judgment of Israel is most severe and God sees no righteous person on the earth.

Psalm 18

Though this psalm contains direct references to David's struggles and subsequent victory, it also applies to the last days. Verses 7–14 of Psalm 18 relate the cataclysmic events surrounding the second coming of Christ and the hour of testing upon the earth. Then, verses 16 and 19 describe the rapture in poetic terms: "He reached down from on high and took hold of me; he drew me out of deep waters. . . . He brought me out into a spacious place; he rescued me because he delighted in me." Last, verse 24 refers to the judgment of the saints: "The Lord has rewarded me according to my righteousness."

Psalm 21

Psalm 21:9–10 states, "At the time of your appearing you will make them like a fiery furnace. In his wrath the LORD will swallow them up, and his fire will consume them. You will destroy their descendants from the earth, their posterity from mankind."

Here God is equating his second coming to his "appearing," where his wrath is being unleashed on the earth. Only Christians will be allowed to enter the millennial kingdom, so the posterity of the wicked will literally be removed from the earth.

Psalms 27 and 46

Psalm 27:5 also has last-days implications. After discussing God's protection of the remnant of Israel during the hour of testing, David wrote, "In the day of trouble he will keep me safe in his dwelling; he will hide me in the shelter of his tabernacle and set me high upon a rock." Psalm 46:2 states, "Therefore we will not fear, though the earth give way and the mountains fall into the heart of the sea."

Psalm 50

Psalm 50:3–7 discusses the second coming of Christ, his wrath upon the earth, and the judging of the saints:

> Our God comes and will not be silent; a fire devours
> before him, and around him a tempest rages. He

summons the heavens above, and the earth, that he may judge his people: "Gather to me my consecrated ones, who made a covenant with me by sacrifice." And the heavens proclaim his righteousness, for God himself is judge. *Selah.*

"Hear, O my people, and I will speak, O Israel, and I will testify against you: I am God, your God."

Verses 14–15 say, "Sacrifice thank offerings to God, fulfill your vows to the Most High, and call upon me in the day of trouble." God is again asking the remnant of Israel who are there during "Jacob's trouble" to return to him.

Psalm 110

Psalm 110:1–2 says, "The LORD says to my Lord: 'Sit at my right hand until I make your enemies a footstool for your feet.' The LORD will extend your mighty scepter from Zion; you will rule in the midst of your enemies." Since Christ's ascension into heaven he has remained at the right hand of God, and his enemies will not be made his footstool (see Isa. 66:1; Matt. 5:35; Acts 7:49; Heb. 1:13; 10:12–13) until he returns to Mount Zion at his second coming. He will then unleash his wrath upon all the earth during the hour of testing, and this will be followed closely by his millennium kingdom rule.

Verses 5–6 state, "The Lord is at your right hand; he will crush kings on the day of his wrath. He will judge the nations, heaping up the dead." This is surely in reference to the battle of Armageddon. So these verses contradict the view of a rapture at the beginning of the tribulation, because Christ would not have made his enemies a footstool until near the end of the tribulation. A pretribulation rapture would require Christ to leave the right hand of God to rapture the church, return to the right hand of God, and later go back to earth to make his enemies a footstool. This would, in essence, create a third coming of Christ, which would be another contradiction of Scripture, to say the least. But a rapture at the second coming fits perfectly into this prophecy.

Chapter 14

WHAT THE PROPHET ISAIAH
SAID ABOUT THE TIMING OF THE
RAPTURE

The prophet Isaiah wrote much about the rapture of the church in conjunction with the second coming of Christ. Let's look at four major passages.

Isaiah 40

When Christ comes to reward the saints at the rapture, he will not come secretly. Rather, the whole world will know. It would be an insult for anyone to think that Jesus, in all his glory, would come secretly for the church.

> Every valley shall be raised up, every mountain and hill made low; the rough ground shall become level, the rugged places a plain. And the glory of the LORD will be revealed, and all mankind together will see it . . . See, the Sovereign LORD comes with power, and his arm rules for him. See, his reward is with him, and his recompense accompanies him.
>
> —Isa. 40:4–5, 10

The "recompense" involves the judgments of the earth at Christ's second coming, but the "reward" is the rapture. So, at the same time the saints are raptured, the wrath of God is coming down on planet earth.

Isaiah 41

Isaiah 41:1, 4–5 says,

> Be silent before me, you islands! Let the nations renew their strength! Let them come forward and speak; let us meet together at the place of judgment. . . . Who has done this and carried it through, calling forth the generations from the beginning? I, the LORD—with the first of them and with the last—I am he. The islands have seen it and fear; the ends of the earth tremble.

Clearly this passage explains the rapture and second coming. The "generations from the beginning" are the Christians who will be called to judgment, which occurs immediately after the rapture.

Isaiah 60

In Isaiah 60:1–2, 5a, 8 we read,

> Arise, shine, for your light has come, and the glory of the LORD rises upon you. See, darkness covers the earth and thick darkness is over the peoples, but the LORD rises upon you and his glory appears over you. . . . Then you will look and be radiant, your heart will throb and swell with joy; . . . Who are these that fly along like clouds, like doves to their nests?

Though this passage has primary application to the nation Israel, you can still see references to the raptured saints, who will be radiant and will soar like eagles. The earth, however, will be covered in darkness, associated with the second-coming judgments of God.

Isaiah 62

Isaiah 62:11–12 reads as follows:

> The LORD has made proclamation to the ends of the earth: "Say to the Daughter of Zion, 'See, your Savior

comes! See, his reward is with him, and his recompense
accompanies him.'" They will be called the Holy People,
the Redeemed of the LORD; and you will be called
Sought After, the City No Longer Deserted.

The glorified saints at the rapture will have new names that describe
their character and their standing before God: "the Holy People" and
"Redeemed of the LORD." The nation of Israel will be "Sought After,"
and Jerusalem will be "the City No Longer Deserted" during the millennial kingdom.

Chapter 15

Let's turn now to what Jesus said about his second coming and the rapture of the church. Such discussion should also verify the timing of these events.

In Matthew 24:3, Jesus' disciples asked him, "What will be the sign of your coming and of the end of the age?" Jesus told them they could expect deceitful people claiming to be Christ, "wars and rumors of wars," "famines and earthquakes in various places," and persecution (Matt. 24:4–10). Then he offered hope for the Christians:

> At that time the sign of the Son of Man will appear in the sky, and all the nations of the earth will mourn. They will see the Son of Man coming on the clouds of the sky, with power and great glory. And he will send his angels with a loud trumpet call, and they will gather his elect from the four winds, from one end of the heavens to the other.
>
> —Matt. 24:30–31; see Mark 13:26–27

This passage clearly groups the second coming of Christ with the rapture of the church.

Then in Matthew 24:37–41, Jesus says,

> As it was in the days of Noah, so it will be at the coming of the Son of Man. For in the days before the flood, people were eating and drinking, marrying and giving

in marriage, up to the day Noah entered the ark; and they knew nothing about what would happen until the flood came and took them all away. That is how it will be at the coming of the Son of Man. Two men will be in the field; one will be taken and the other left. Two women will be grinding with a hand mill; one will be taken and the other left.

—See Luke 17:30–36

In the same setting Jesus references those "being taken" in conjunction with the rapture, which occurs at the second coming.

In Luke 21:26–27, a parallel passage to Matthew 24, we read these words of Jesus:

Men will faint from terror, apprehensive of what is coming on the world, for the heavenly bodies will be shaken. At that time they will see the Son of Man coming in a cloud with power and great glory. When these things begin to take place, stand up and lift up your heads, because your redemption is drawing nearer.

Cataclysmic events occur with the second coming and the "redemption" Jesus referred to is the rapture of the church, in which we are redeemed from the earth and glorified for the whole world to see.

Chapter 16

Beyond the Gospels, the New Testament letters of Paul, the writer of Hebrews, James, Peter, and Jude give much support to the concept of the rapture occurring at the second coming.

Romans

In Romans 2, we read,

> Because of your stubbornness and your unrepentant heart, you are storing up wrath against yourself for the day of God's wrath, when his righteous judgment will be revealed. God "will give to each person according to what he has done." To those who by persistence in doing good seek glory, honor and immortality, he will give eternal life. But for those who are self-seeking and who reject the truth and follow evil, there will be wrath and anger.
>
> —Rom. 2:5–8

The day of wrath comes for unbelievers at their death, or the second coming of Christ, if they are unfortunate enough to be alive at that time. The same "day of God's wrath" is the day of the "righteous judgment" for the saints who are alive at the glorious time of the second coming, and for all who died in Christ prior to that time.

Romans 8:18–24 says,

> I consider that our present sufferings are not worth comparing with the glory that will be revealed in us. The creation waits in eager expectation for the sons of God to be revealed. For the creation was subjected to frustration, not by its own choice, but by the will of the one who subjected it, in hope that the creation itself will be liberated from its bondage to decay and brought into the glorious freedom of the children of God. We know that the whole creation has been groaning as in the pains of childbirth right up to the present time. Not only so, but we ourselves, who have the firstfruits of the Spirit, groan inwardly as we wait eagerly for our adoption as sons, the redemption of our bodies.

The "glory that will be revealed" is the rapture or "the redemption of our bodies." It's important to note that when Christ is revealed at his second coming, the whole world will know, and they will also see us in all our glory.

Romans 13:11–12 states, "And do this, understanding the present time. The hour has come for you to wake up from your slumber, because our salvation is nearer now than when we first believed. The night is nearly over; the day is almost here." We need to understand the signs of the times, and many Christians in America today need to "wake up" from their spiritual slumber. Our redemption is drawing nearer, but Christians must first experience the night of the tribulation before we experience the glorious second coming.

1 and 2 Corinthians

The apostle Paul, through the divine inspiration of the Holy Spirit, had much to say to the church at Corinth (and us!) about the timing of the rapture.

First Corinthians 3:13 says every person's "work will be shown for what it is, because the Day will bring it to light. It will be revealed with fire, and the fire will test the quality of each man's work." The "Day" in this verse refers to the day of the Lord or the second coming, which is when the judgment of the saints occurs after the rapture. Fire is used to judge the earth as well as the righteous works of the saints.

First Corinthians 4:5 tells us, "Therefore judge nothing before the appointed time; wait till the Lord comes. He will bring to light what is hidden in darkness and will expose the motives of men's hearts. At that time each will receive his praise from God." The Lord Jesus Christ will return at the second coming to reward the saints with the rapture, and their works will be judged. The unsaved world, however, will be shown the wrath of God; and, a thousand years later, they will be judged at the great white throne judgment.

Paul was addressing what to do with a brother who was caught in sexual immorality when he wrote, "hand this man over to Satan, so that the sinful nature may be destroyed and his spirit saved on the day of the Lord" (1 Cor. 5:5). The day of the Lord is the second coming of Christ, and that is when our redemption is complete.

In chapter 15, Paul wrote about the significance of the resurrection of Christ:

> But Christ has indeed been raised from the dead, the firstfruits of those who have fallen asleep. For since death came through a man, the resurrection of the dead comes also through a man. For as in Adam all die, so in Christ all will be made alive. But each in his own turn: Christ, the firstfruits; then, when he comes, those who belong to him.
>
> —1 Cor. 15:20–23

Christ is the first to resurrect in a glorified body, but we will likewise be resurrected "when he comes." And, when he comes, he will be here to stay—not sneaking back to heaven, but bringing heaven with him to earth at Mount Zion.

Moving into 2 Corinthians, we read in chapter 1 verse 14, "as you have understood us in part, you will come to understand fully that you can boast of us just as we will boast of you in the day of the Lord Jesus." We will understand all things fully in our glorified state at the rapture, and we will boast in the day of the Lord, which is his second coming.

We will have nothing to boast about seven years earlier—except that Jesus will give us the strength to get through the tribulation.

Ephesians

In Ephesians the rapture is addressed in several places.

Ephesians 2:5 says God "made us alive with Christ even when we were dead in transgressions—it is by grace that you have been saved." And though we are "seated . . . with [Christ] in the heavenly realms" (Eph. 2:6) at our point of conversion, we are also "sealed for the day of redemption" (Eph. 4:30).

At the second coming, Ephesians 5:14 will be completely fulfilled: "for it is light that makes everything visible. This is why it is said: 'Wake up, O sleeper, rise from the dead, and Christ will shine on you.'" Christ is coming, so we need to wake up and be about God's business now. The evil darkness of the world will be revealed for what it is, and God's wrath will be displayed on the very same day he raptures the saints.

Philippians

Philippians 1:6 says, "being confident of this, that he who began a good work in you will carry it on to completion until the day of Christ Jesus." Our good works are complete at the second coming, because on that day we are glorified.

Verse 10 states, "so that you may be able to discern what is best and may be pure and blameless until the day of Christ."

Then in verses 27–28 we read,

> Whatever happens, conduct yourselves in a manner worthy of the gospel of Christ. Then, whether I come and see you or only hear about you in my absence, I will know that you stand firm in one spirit, contending as one man for the faith of the gospel without being frightened in any way by those who oppose you. This is a sign to them that they will be destroyed, but that you will be saved—and that by God.

Our lives may be difficult in the tribulation, but the "sign" will be fulfilled when we are raptured at the second coming.

Philippians 2:14–16 says,

> Do everything without complaining or arguing, so that you may be blameless and pure, children of God without fault in a crooked and depraved generation, in which you shine like stars in the universe as you hold out the word of life—in order that I may boast on the day of Christ that I did not run or labor for nothing.

So what would there be to boast about at the second coming, if Christ is only coming to destroy the world? But, if that very same day is associated with the rapture, then there is indeed reason to boast, as we will be in our glorified state. What an awesome day the second coming will be for us, as we are glorified and boast in his glory and eternal reward!

Colossians

Colossians 1:19–20 says, "God was pleased to have all his fullness dwell in [Christ], and through him to reconcile to himself all things, whether things on earth or things in heaven, by making peace through his blood, shed on the cross." At conversion we are reconciled to Christ, but the complete fulfillment of that reconciliation occurs at our glorification, when our bodies are completely free from sin.

Colossians 3:4 offers this hope: "When Christ, who is your life appears, then you also will appear with him in glory." Our glorification becomes a reality at the second coming, when the Lord Jesus "appears" to the whole world—and it will not occur in secret.

1 Thessalonians

First Thessalonians 1:10 states: "and to wait for his Son from heaven, whom he raised from the dead—Jesus, who rescues us from the coming wrath." Jesus indeed rescues all who die in him from the coming wrath of hell, and later gehenna. Jesus will also rescue the tribulation saints from the wrath of the second coming, through their rapture.

First Thessalonians 2:19 states: "For what is our hope, our joy, or the crown in which we will glory in the presence of our Lord Jesus when he comes?" Paul knew he would receive the "crown of glory" at the rapture, when Jesus returns at his second coming.

First Thessalonians 3:13 states: "May he strengthen your hearts so that you will be blameless and holy in the presence of our God and Father when our Lord Jesus comes with all his holy ones." Jesus comes with all his angels or "holy ones" referenced here, at the second coming. At this time we will be completely holy and blameless in our resurrection bodies.

A distinctive group of verses in chapters 4 and 5 clearly links the rapture with the second coming, beginning with a description of the rapture:

> Brothers, we do not want you to be ignorant about those who fall asleep, or to grieve like the rest of men, who have no hope. We believe that Jesus died and rose again and so we believe that God will bring with Jesus those who have fallen asleep in him. According to the Lord's own word, we tell you that we who are still alive, who are left till the coming of the Lord, will certainly not precede those who have fallen asleep. For the Lord himself will come down from heaven, with a loud command, with the voice of the archangel and with the trumpet call of God, and the dead in Christ will rise first. After that, we who are still alive and are left will be caught up together with them in the clouds to meet the Lord in the air. And so we will be with the Lord forever. Therefore encourage each other with these words.
>
> —1 Thess. 14:13–18

Paul then used a "transition participle" in 5:1 to make clear that he was talking about a contiguous series of events—the rapture and the second coming: "Now, brothers, about times and dates we do not need to write to you, for you know very well that the day of the Lord will come like a thief in the night. While people are saying, 'Peace and safety,' destruction will come on them suddenly, as labor pains on a pregnant woman, and they will not escape" (1 Thess. 5:1–3).

Next Paul went on to show that the day of the Lord (his second coming) will be a different experience for true Christians, since it will not be unexpected.

> But you, brothers, are not in darkness so that this day should surprise you like a thief. You are all sons of the light and sons of the day. We do not belong to the night or to the darkness. So then, let us not be like others, who are asleep, but let us be alert and self-controlled. For those who sleep, sleep at night, and those who get drunk, get drunk at night. But since we belong to the day, let us be self-controlled, putting on faith and love as a breastplate, and the hope of salvation as a helmet. For God did not appoint us to suffer wrath but to receive salvation through our Lord Jesus Christ. He died for us so that, whether we are awake or asleep, we may live together with him. Therefore encourage one another and build each other up, just as in fact you are doing.
> —1 Thess. 5:4–11

Clearly, the day of the Lord is a day of glory and bright light for the saved, because they are being raptured, whereas the unsaved are in darkness and misery, as the final hour of God's wrath is being poured out against them.

The letters to the Thessalonians were written to Christians, so it seems clear that Paul expected many believers to experience the tribulation, though he offered hope because of the ultimate glory and rescue they will have at the second coming and rapture.

Incidentally, the Greek word *apantesis*, used in 1 Thessalonians 4:17 of believers being "caught up" to meet the Lord in the air, settles the whole debate about the rapture. This word means to "meet and continue on in the direction that the person being met is going," and it is used in two other places in Scripture. In Acts 28:15 the apostles were going to meet Paul and accompany him as he was going to Rome. In Matthew 25:6 the ten virgins were waiting for the bridegroom to arrive so they could follow him to the bride's house. In both references individuals go from point A to meet the others at point B, and then all go to point C. Christ is at point A, at the right hand of God in heaven prior to the rapture. He meets the church at point B, which is in the air at the rapture. They all go on to point C, which is on Mount Zion. Christ brings heaven and all the raptured saints to earth onto Mount Zion at the second coming. *Apantesis* does not mean to meet the Lord and go back with him to where he came from. In a pretribulation rapture, Jesus would go from point A to point B to rapture the church, and then back to point A. Psalm 110:1 says, "The LORD says to my Lord, 'Sit at my right hand until I make your enemies a footstool for your feet.'" Jesus will not leave the right hand of the Father until he raptures the church on his way to Mount Zion, where he will make the earth his "footstool." And without a doubt, Jesus' trip to Zion will not take seven years!

2 Thessalonians

One of the main reasons Paul wrote his second letter to the Thessalonians was to dispel the false doctrine that the second coming and rapture had already occurred. Because they faced extreme persecution, some of the Thessalonians believed they had missed the rapture. So Paul wrote,

> Concerning the *coming of our Lord Jesus Christ* and *our being gathered to him*, we ask you, brothers, not to become easily unsettled or alarmed by some prophecy, report or letter supposed to have come from us, saying that the *day of the Lord* has already come. Don't let anyone deceive you in any way, for *that day* will not come until the rebellion occurs and the man of lawlessness is revealed, the man doomed for destruction.
> —2 Thess. 2:1–3 (emphasis added)

It is interesting how the "coming of our Lord" and the "day of the Lord" are grouped with the rapture, or "our being gathered to him," verifying that these events occur together. Note that the "day" mentioned in verse 4 is a specific day for this cluster of events.

Paul surely supports this view of the rapture and second coming being a single event also in 2 Thessalonians 1:7–10:

> . . . when the Lord Jesus is revealed from heaven in blazing fire with his powerful angels. He will punish those who do not know God and do not obey the gospel of our Lord Jesus. They will be punished with everlasting destruction and shut out from the presence of the Lord and from the majesty of his power on the day he comes to be glorified in his holy people and to be marveled at among all those who have believed.

God's people are glorified at the rapture, which is discussed in the context of the second coming.

1 Timothy

In 1 Timothy 6:13–16 we read,

> I charge you to keep this command without spot or blame until the appearing of our Lord Jesus Christ, which God will bring about in his own time—God, the blessed and only Ruler, the King of kings and Lord of lords, who alone is immortal and who lives in unapproachable light, whom no one has seen or can see. To him be honor and might forever. Amen.

Jesus will come at the end of this age to set up his kingdom. We are "without spot or blame" in the spiritual sense, because of the blood of Christ shed for our sins. The ultimate fulfillment of our bodies being without spot or blemish will be at the second coming and the associated rapture.

2 Timothy

In 2 Timothy 1:12, the apostle Paul said he was not ashamed of his suffering for the gospel, because he was convinced the Lord was "able to guard what I have entrusted to him for that day." We, too, have entrusted our bodies to Christ, and "that day" is the day of the Lord, where these bodies are glorified.

In verse 18, Paul was interceding for the "household of Onesiphorus," asking God to show them mercy on the day he judges the saints, at the second coming or day of the Lord. He wrote, "May the Lord grant that he will find mercy from the Lord on that day!"

Second Timothy 4:1 says, "In the presence of God and of Christ Jesus, who will judge the living and the dead, and in view of his appearing and his kingdom, I give you this charge." The Greek word used for "appearing" is *epiphaneia*, which means "manifestation or advent of Christ or his appearing or brightness," and from which we get our English word *epiphany*. So Christ will judge the living and the dead at the rapture of his saints in conjunction with the appearing of the Lord.

To encourage Timothy, as well as his other readers, Paul wrote, "Now there is in store for me the crown of righteousness, which the Lord, the righteous Judge, will award to me on that day—and not only to me, but also to all who have longed for his appearing" (2 Tim. 4:8). The saints in the tribulation will face difficult circumstances due to their faith, so they will definitely be longing "for his appearing," if they are living without compromise. The award of the "crown of righteousness" will be given on the day of judgment to all the saints who have persevered in generations past and present—not placing their hope in the world or themselves, but looking for the second coming of Christ.

Titus

Titus 2:12–13 states, "It [the grace of God] teaches us to say 'No' to ungodliness and worldly passions, and to live self-controlled, upright and godly lives in this present age, while we wait for the blessed hope—the glorious appearing of our great God and Savior, Jesus Christ." The present age ends at the second coming of Christ, and his glorious appearing is our hope, since all believers will be glorified at that point.

Hebrews

The writer to the Hebrews said, "Christ was sacrificed once to take away the sins of many people; and he will appear a second time, not to bear sin, but to bring salvation to those who are waiting for him" (Heb. 9:28). It is at the second coming that those who are waiting for him will find their salvation complete at the rapture.

Hebrews 10:25 tells us to not stop meeting together with Christians on a regular basis, especially "as you see the Day approaching." That "Day" is the day of the Lord, the second coming of Christ.

James

James 5:7–9 says,

> Be patient, then, brothers, until the Lord's coming. See how the farmer waits for the land to yield its valuable crop and how patient he is for the autumn and spring rains. You too, be patient and stand firm, because the Lord's coming is near. Don't grumble against each other, brothers, or you will be judged. The Judge is standing at the door!

The Greek word for "coming" used here is *parousia*, which means "advent or return or coming near." This is not a secret return we are waiting for, but a glorious unveiling or revelation that the whole world will see—the time of the harvest and the judgment of the saints that happens at the second coming, not seven years earlier.

1 Peter

First Peter 1:3–5 states,

> Praise be to the God and Father of our Lord Jesus Christ! In his great mercy he has given us new birth into a living hope through the resurrection of Jesus Christ from the dead, and into an inheritance that can never perish, spoil or fade—kept in heaven for you,

who through faith are shielded by God's power until the coming of the salvation that is ready to be revealed in the last time.

Verse 13 says, "Therefore, prepare your minds for action; be self-controlled; set your hope fully on the grace to be given you when Jesus Christ is revealed." The Greek word for "revealed" used in these verses is *apokalupto*, which means to "take off the cover." Jesus will be fully unveiled at the second coming, and that is the time of our grace and glorification. The whole world will see that revelation, and there is no hint of anything secretive.

In 2:12, Peter wrote, "Live such good lives among the pagans that, though they accuse you of doing wrong, they may see your good deeds and glorify God on the day he visits us." When Jesus "visits us," he will be here to stay, and our witness to those who come to Christ will all be to God's glory at the second coming.

Other verses in 1 Peter that support the rapture occurring at the second coming are as follows:

- "But rejoice that you participate in the sufferings of Christ, so that you may be overjoyed when his glory is revealed" (1 Pet. 4:13).
- "To the elders among you, I appeal as a fellow elder, a witness of Christ's sufferings and one who also will share in the glory to be revealed" (1 Pet. 5:1).
- "And when the Chief Shepherd appears, you will receive the crown of glory that will never fade away" (1 Pet. 5:4).

2 Peter

In Peter's second letter, we read the following: "And we have the word of the prophets made more certain, and you will do well to pay attention to it, as to a light shining in the dark place, until the day dawns and the morning star rises in your hearts" (2 Pet. 1:19). The "morning star" is the second coming of Christ Jesus that will occur near the end of the tribulation, when darkness will cover the earth. The whole world will see that light.

Second Peter 2:9 states, "if this is so, then the Lord knows how to rescue godly men from trials and to hold the unrighteous for the day of judgment, while continuing their punishment." We will be rescued at the rapture, which will be the same day the second-coming judgments will begin on the earth.

Jude

In verses 14–15, 18, and 21 of Jude, we read,

> See, the Lord is coming with thousands upon thousands of his holy ones to judge everyone, and to convict all the ungodly of all the ungodly acts they have done in the ungodly way, and of all the harsh words ungodly sinners have spoken against him. . . . In the last times there will be scoffers who will follow their own ungodly desires. . . . Keep yourselves in God's love as you wait for the mercy of our Lord Jesus Christ to bring you to eternal life.

There will be a day of judgment when the earth is judged with fire, even though talk of the second coming has gone on for centuries, and scoffers continue to do their thing. But the mercy of God brings us, his children, to eternal life at his coming.

PART 3
MAJOR PEOPLE AND EVENTS
OF THE END TIMES

Chapter 17

Without a doubt, the most intriguing—and perhaps the most frightening—person involved in the end times is the Antichrist. We can barely imagine someone so totally devoted to evil, someone so completely set on destroying Christianity and its adherents. However, the Bible leaves no doubt that this person will exist and will essentially rule the world—for a time. But where will he come from? Let's see what the Scriptures have to say about the origins of the "Beast."

Gentile or Jew?

I firmly believe the Antichrist will be a Jew, based in part on Daniel 11:36–39 (KJV):

> The king shall do according to his will; and he shall exalt himself, and magnify himself above every god, and shall speak marvelous things against the God of gods, and shall prosper till the indignation be accomplished: for that that is determined shall be done. Neither shall he regard the God of his fathers, nor the desire of women, nor regard any god: for he shall magnify himself above all. But in his estate shall he honour the God of forces: and a god whom his fathers knew not shall he honour with gold, and silver, and with precious stones, and pleasant things. Thus shall he do in the most strong holds with a strange god, whom he shall acknowledge

and increase with glory: and he shall cause them to rule over many, and shall divide the land for gain.

Verse 37 says the Antichrist will not follow the "God of his fathers"—*Elohim* in Hebrew—referring to the one true God of his Jewish fathers. Some scholars believe the word describes plural "gods," but *Elohim* most often refers to one God, and verse 36 clarifies: "God of gods."

Not only does he not follow God, the Antichrist exalts *himself* as god (verse 37) and gives honor to the "god of forces" (verse 38), which is none other than Satan. Then he encourages others to worship this "strange god," so called because Satan has never been worshiped directly, in any organized way, by Jewish people. As a result, Satan helps the Antichrist win various battles and take control of the world. Such an interpretation of Daniel 11 agrees with Revelation 13:2: "The dragon [Satan] gave the beast [Antichrist] his power and his throne and great authority."

Some believe that the reference to the Beast or Antichrist coming "out of the sea" (Rev. 13:1) implies he will be a Gentile, but I believe the "sea" here stands for the nations of the world, or the unrighteousness of humanity, with no religious direction.

A Worthless Shepherd

Zechariah 11 gives us more insight into the origin of the Antichrist. Verse 16 says, "For I am going to raise up a shepherd over the land who will not care for the lost, or seek the young, or heal the injured, or feed the healthy, but will eat the meat of the choice sheep, tearing off their hoofs." This last shepherd for Israel is none other than the Antichrist. It is implied that he is Jewish, since a Jewish person would be the most likely to watch over the sheep of Israel.

In Revelation 13:3 we read of the Antichrist's "fatal wound" that has been healed, and in verse 14 we learn how he will receive it: "the beast who was wounded by the sword and yet lived."

The fatal wound is also referenced in Zechariah 11:17: "Woe to the worthless shepherd, who deserts the flock! May the sword strike his arm and his right eye! May his arm be completely withered, his right eye totally blinded!" The Antichrist will likely be stabbed in the eye, penetrating into his skull. His arm will also be severely damaged. He will desert the flock of Israel at the midpoint of the tribulation, when the slaughter of the Jews will start. Interestingly, since the Antichrist will neither watch over the sheep of Israel nor provide protection, God's judgment will appropriately focus on these two areas of his body that are used to fulfill these neglected responsibilities: the eye and right arm.

The Antichrist is not the only one who will abandon the sheep of Israel in the last days. Verses 4–5 read, "This is what the LORD my God says: 'Pasture the flock marked for slaughter. Their buyers slaughter them and go unpunished. Those who sell them say, "Praise the LORD, I am rich!" Their own shepherds do not spare them.'" It appears that the spiritual leaders turn over their own people who are not willing to submit to the Antichrist.

The sheep marked for slaughter were purchased for "thirty pieces of silver" (Zech. 11:12)—the same price Judas Iscariot was paid for betraying Jesus (Matt. 26:15). Judas and the Antichrist share many similarities: Both are betrayers; both are Jews; both will have been indwelt by Satan at some point in their lives (John 13:26); and both come to ultimate destruction.

From the Tribe of Dan

Not only do I believe the Antichrist will be a Jew, but more specifically, he will come from the tribe of Dan. Deuteronomy 33:22 states, "Dan is a lion's cub, springing out of Bashan." When the Israelites first settled the Promised Land, Bashan was a fertile area in the north whose border reached into Mount Hermon. Today the land is in Syria. In the Bible, Bashan often symbolizes worldly prosperity that results from arrogant pride and selfish indulgence. For example, "Hear this word, you cows of Bashan on Mount Samaria, you women who oppress the poor and crush the needy and say to your husbands 'Bring us some drinks!'" (Amos 4:1).

Psalm 22 is a prophetic psalm that includes many references to Jesus' crucifixion (verses 1, 7, 14, 16, 18), including verses 12–13: "Many bulls surround me; strong bulls of Bashan encircle me. Roaring lions tearing their prey open their mouths wide against me." The "strong bulls of Bashan" represent the worldly and satanic forces instrumental in Christ's crucifixion.

In the last days, once again the "lion cub" (Deut. 33:22), Dan, will come from Bashan, "springing out" against Israel, and later against Christ after his second coming, when the Antichrist will organize the forces that war in the battle of Armageddon. Since the Antichrist is from Dan, his forces are classified as coming from Bashan in the following passage:

> A voice is announcing from Dan, proclaiming disaster from the hills of Ephraim. "Tell this to the nations, proclaim it to Jerusalem: 'A besieging army is coming from a distant land, raising a war cry against the cities of Judah. They surround her like men guarding a field, because she has rebelled against me,'" declares the LORD. . . .
>
> I looked at the mountains, and they were quaking; all the hills were swaying. I looked, and there were no people; every bird in the sky had flown away. I looked, and the fruitful land was a desert; all its towns lay in ruins before the LORD, before his fierce anger.
>
> This is what the LORD says: "The whole land will be ruined, though I will not destroy it completely."
> —Jer. 4:15–17, 24–27

This reference in Jeremiah is a telescoping prophecy, dealing with the impending invasion of the Babylonian Empire through Dan, and also with the final Babylonian Empire (see Rev. 18), which will fall after it attempts to conquer the nation Israel through Dan. Jeremiah 8:16–20 also mentions the enemy coming from Dan. Verse 20 says, "The harvest is past, the summer has ended, and we are not saved," referring to the time after the rapture, when Israel is still in ignorance.

Dan and his animals are ultimately defeated at the battle of Armageddon as referenced in this passage:

> Son of man, this is what the Sovereign LORD says:
> Call out to every kind of bird and all the wild animals:
> "Assemble and come together from all around to the
> sacrifice I am preparing for you, the great sacrifice on
> the mountains of Israel. There you will eat flesh and
> drink blood. You will eat the flesh of mighty men and
> drink the blood of the princes of the earth as if they
> were rams and lambs, goats and bulls—all of them fat-
> tened animals from Bashan."
>
> —Ezek. 39:17–20

Another aspect of the tribe of Dan is its promotion of idol worship. (See 1 Kings 12:28–30; Judg. 18:18, 30–31.) This was indeed an
abomination to God. It would seem logical that influence from Dan
would be big in the idolatry of the end-times world system represented
by the last Babylon (Rev. 18). Amos 8:9–14 addresses the day of the
Lord with verse 14 saying, "They who swear by the shame of Samaria,
or say, 'As surely as your god lives, O Dan,' or, 'As surely as the god
of Beersheba lives'—they will fall, never to rise again." Samaria, Dan,
and Beersheba were centers of idol worship whose people, even in the
future, will be upset that their false gods will not protect them from the
wrath of God revealed at his second coming.

Because of Dan's idolatry, they are not represented in the 144,000
witnesses (Rev. 7). Fortunately for this tribe, however, they are represented in the final millennial kingdom lineage (Ezek. 48:1–2).

Another earlier passage supports the Antichrist coming from the
tribe of Dan. Genesis 49:16–17 (KJV) says, "Dan shall judge his people,
as one of the tribes of Israel. Dan shall be a serpent by the way, an
adder in the path, that biteth the horse heels, so that his rider shall
fall backward. Oh, how I have waited for thy salvation, O Lord." The
"serpent" is Satan, and it is he who controls the Antichrist, who comes
from the tribe of Dan. Within the context of these verses, the meaning
of the Hebrew word for "judge" (*diyn*) conveys a negative and harsh
judgment, using an instrument of wrath. Some falsely believe Samson,
who came from the tribe of Dan, fulfilled this prophecy, but Samson
did not rule like a serpent. (See Judg. 13:1–16:31.) This passage in
Genesis could also be a prophetic word about the Antichrist's death,

when the serpent (Satan) bites the horse's heel, which may be one of the horses of Apocalypse, when ridden by the Antichrist as he suffers the fatal wound. Satan will orchestrate the death of the Antichrist so that he can later indwell him when he is released from the Abyss. So when the Antichrist rides the pale horse of the Apocalypse, it is really Satan, represented by "Death and Hades" (Rev. 6:8), who is in complete control.

The Genesis 49:18 prophecy fittingly ends with the words, "I have waited for thy salvation, O LORD." The second coming of Jesus is what the world really needs as the answer to its problems from Antichrist's rule and Satan's ultimate control in the last days.

Chapter 18

THE ANTICHRIST AND THE FOUR
HORSES OF THE APOCALYPSE

Though, as we discovered in the last chapter, the Antichrist will be a "worthless shepherd," I believe he will be an accomplished horseman—figuratively speaking, of course. Let's look now at Revelation 6 to learn more about the four horses of the apocalypse and their rider.

The Rider of the White Horse

In Revelation 6:2, John described the rider: "Its rider held a bow, and he was given a crown, and he rode out as a conqueror bent on conquest." Some speculate this is Christ himself. But it doesn't make sense that Christ would be "bent on conquest" at the beginning of the tribulation, when the great "falling away" (2 Thess. 2:3 KJV) from the faith will be occurring and during which there will be a "famine of the word of God" (Amos 8:11). The time for Christ to conquer is at the second coming, where he makes his enemies his footstool (Ps. 110:1; Heb. 10:12–13). And though Jesus will wear a crown when he shows himself in the tribulation (Rev. 19:12), it will be a *diadem*, a crown of royalty. The Greek word for crown used in verse 2, however, is the same word also used to describe Jesus' crown of thorns (*stephanos*), which he will certainly never wear again (Matt. 27:29; Mark 15:17; John 19:2, 5).

For these reasons, I believe the rider of the white horse—and all the other horses at various points in the tribulation—is the Antichrist. He will begin as a political conqueror—coming in the name of peace—rather than a warring conqueror. That is why the rider has a bow but no arrows. Later on in the tribulation, the bow becomes armed, as he attains greater and still greater power. The Antichrist will relish mimicking Christ, so he comes wearing a crown and riding a white horse, as Jesus will do at the end of the tribulation (Ps. 45:4; Hab. 3:8–15; Rev. 19:11). The Antichrist will ride the white horse—until he reaches near his pinnacle of world control and no longer needs that horse.

The White Horse

Some postulate the actual white horse and its rider represent America and its president, because America is bent on political conquest and the spread of democracy and peace. However, I don't see America anywhere in end-times Bible prophecy. Others believe the white horse is the United Nations or a conglomerate of world superpowers. There are a seemingly infinite number of theories on the identities of all four horses of the apocalypse, but at this point in time it's really impossible to know for certain who or what the white horse symbolizes. I do, however, feel confident that the rider of this horse is none other than the Antichrist.

The Red Horse

With the opening of the second seal, the "red horse," John saw that its rider "was given power to take peace from the earth and to make men slay each other. To him was given a large sword" (Rev. 6:3). If we are indeed on the brink of the tribulation, then I would postulate the current worldwide terrorist movement as the red horse. Are terrorists not the ones causing men to "slay each other," and isn't this movement taking peace from the world? Aren't the descendents of Esau the Palestinian nations? Didn't the contemporary terrorist movement start in Palestine? Esau is referred to as "red" in Genesis 25:25 as follows: "The first to come out was red, and his whole body was like a hairy garment; so they named him Esau." Also, the descendants of Esau were known as "Edomites," meaning red. Could not the "big sword" (Rev. 6:3) be a metaphor for a nuclear weapon that may soon be in the hands of terrorists? It's not impossible to imagine the Antichrist riding the red horse without the world realizing he's the one who is empowering the terrorist movement. He may then stay on the horse until he squashes the movement by implementing the single monetary system (Rev. 13:15–18). After terrorists get nuclear weapons, the world will need to track all financial transactions through the "mark of the beast." With implementation of such a system, financial support for the terrorist movement will soon collapse and the Antichrist will take all the glory—after he gets off the red horse, of course.

If we are indeed in the last days, then the red horse has been let out of the barn, and its rider likely is poised and ready to mount up.

The Black Horse

If terrorism is indeed the red horse, then it is conceivable that the world's superpowers would shift large amounts of money toward fighting it, likely at the expense of feeding the world's poor. As a result, the third seal, the "black horse," may be opened: widespread famine. The rider of the black horse "was holding a pair of scales in his hand. Then I heard what sounded like a voice among the four living creatures, saying, 'A quart of wheat for a day's wages, and three quarts of barley for a day's wages, and do not damage the oil and the wine!' The wealthy will do well through the famine, since they will be able to afford the 'oil and wine'" (Rev. 6:5–6).

Though the Antichrist may ride the black horse, the world will not recognize that he is indirectly responsible for the famine. He will, however, use this situation to increase his power and popularity, and will get off the black horse once he has complete world control near the midpoint of the tribulation when he institutes the mark of the Beast.

The Pale Horse

With a worldwide famine resulting from the previous horse and its associated widespread death, we can imagine how the global stage will be set for plagues to follow; infectious organisms grow and multiply in rotting bodies in the streets. So the fourth seal, the "pale horse," is opened at this time. "Its rider was named Death, and Hades was following close behind him" (Rev. 6:8). Here "Death" is clearly Satan, who has indwelled the Antichrist at this point. "Hades" refers to the Antichrist's troops who are "given power over a fourth of the earth to kill by sword, famine and plague, and by the wild beasts of the earth." A majority of those destroyed will be Christians—both Gentile and Jewish. Some of the saints will be placed before wild beasts, reminiscent of first-century Roman persecution.

Once the Antichrist gets complete power and control of the world near the middle of the tribulation, there will likely be relative world peace and prosperity, with the exception of the continuing persecution and killing of Christians and Jews. With no money needed to fight a war on terrorism, resources can now be funneled toward feeding the poor and rebuilding the world's infrastructures. With the single economic system and "mark of the beast," illegal drug dealing will be greatly curtailed. People with the mark can be tracked at all times, which should decrease kidnappings and missing persons. Food will be plentiful, and the associated relative world peace should win over the world to the Antichrist. Considering the Antichrist's miraculous powers, ability to deceive, and charismatic character, it's not too difficult to imagine how he gains control of the world. Of course, the Antichrist may be riding the pale horse once he has complete power, but it is really Satan who is in control of the world.

Timing of the Horses

Whatever your view on the four horses of the apocalypse, most scholars believe they arrive in sequence, starting at the beginning of the tribulation with the white horse, and finishing with the pale horse, which starts at the middle of the tribulation. Jesus said, "You will hear of wars and rumors of wars, but see to it that you are not alarmed. Such things must happen, but the end is still to come. Nation will rise against nation, and kingdom against kingdom. There will be famines and earthquakes in various places. All these are the beginning of birth pains" (Matt. 24:6–8; see also Luke 21:10–11). His reference to the "birth pains" of the tribulation matches up with the consequences of the four horses. If we think of a mother experiencing birth pains, we know those pains begin long before hard labor. Likewise, Israel, which will be "in labor" during the great tribulation, will experience "birth pains" at the beginning of the tribulation, and "hard labor" during the last three-and-a-half years of the tribulation, when the persecution against Israel's elect will intensify. The child metaphorically born from this labor is Jesus, "born" to Israel at his second coming. He will not be crucified this time around, but will save his Jewish people! The joy for Israel's elect will be like that of a mother who has just delivered a beautiful and perfect baby.

Chapter 11

The Antichrist doesn't work alone; he has a "partner in crime," a person the Bible calls the "False Prophet" (Rev. 16:13). The False Prophet will be integral in forcing people to accept the mark of the beast, as well as leading the single world religion, which we will discuss at length in this chapter.

The False Prophet and the Worldwide Religious System

The False Prophet is instrumental in introducing and organizing the worldwide false religious system, the "great prostitute" of Revelation 17:1. The prostitute is the trinity of evil's parody of the church, the body of Christ. As the Holy Spirit is the empowering force within the church, so the False Prophet is within the great prostitute.

The contrast between the church and the great prostitute can be better appreciated by comparing the following two passages, which are visions given by angels holding the bowl judgments.

> One of the seven angels who had the seven bowls came and said to me, "Come, I will show you the punishment of the great prostitute who sits on many waters. With her the kings of the earth committed adultery and the inhabitants of the earth were intoxicated with the wine of her adulteries."
>
> —Rev. 17:1–2

> One of the seven angels who had the seven bowls full of the seven last plagues came and said to me, "Come, I will show you the bride, the wife of the Lamb." And he carried me away in the Spirit to a mountain great and high, and showed me the Holy City, Jerusalem, coming down out of heaven from God.
>
> —Rev. 21:9–10

The prostitute has no legitimate husband and commits adultery in the worship of many false gods. The church, however, is married to Christ alone and is pure and holy. Revelation 17:4–6 says this prostitute was adorned with "gold, precious stones and pearls" and held a "golden cup in her hand, filled with abominable things and the filth of her adulteries." She "was drunk with the blood of the saints," so she is not only the mimic of the church, but also the enemy of the church. In contrast, the church is dressed in humility in her life on earth, but she will be dressed in splendor in the New Jerusalem!

This false religious system will be led by the False Prophet and be implemented near the beginning of the tribulation in an attempt to create world stability. It will be destroyed, however, just prior to the midpoint of the tribulation, likely in conjunction with the Beast coming up out of the Abyss after recovering from the "fatal wound" (Rev. 9:1–2; 11:7; 17:8).

After the fall of the great prostitute, the confederacy of ten kings and the Beast will reign for "one hour" (Rev. 17:12). It is ironic that the forces that help support and carry the great prostitute are the same forces that lead to her destruction:

> The beast and the ten horns you saw will hate the prostitute. They will bring her to ruin and leave her naked; they will eat her flesh and burn her with fire. For God has put it into their hearts to accomplish his purpose by agreeing to give the beast their power to rule, until God's words are fulfilled. The woman you saw is the great city that rules over the kings of the earth.
>
> —Rev. 17:16–18

Notice that this great prostitute has her political and religious center likely in Rome, and will "rule" over the kings of the earth as the sixth world kingdom. (See also Rev. 17:12). So the ten kings will have to destroy the great prostitute before they can rule as kings with the Antichrist, as the seventh kingdom: "The ten horns you saw are ten kings who have not yet received a kingdom, but who for one hour will receive authority as kings along with the beast. They have one purpose and will give their power and authority to the beast" (Rev. 17:12–13). The Beast, then, will rule as the eighth king, until "God's words are fulfilled."

It might seem odd that the False Prophet, the head of the universal religious system, would not be destroyed along with the sixth kingdom. But the False Prophet's true loyalty is not to the religious system, but to the Antichrist and the promotion of Satan's kingdom on earth. So why destroy something so vital to this "trinity of evil"?

The term "Babylon" has symbolized anything that opposes God: the rebellion of the heavenly hosts, the original sin of humankind in the garden of Eden, the rebellion at the Tower of Babel, and all inherent evil worldly kingdoms, including the first and last Babylon. The last Babylon is the culmination of that rebellion that starts at the mid-point of the tribulation after the great prostitute is destroyed, and it is accelerated and expanded when the trinity of evil takes complete control of the world as humanity's obsession with luxury, drunkenness, homosexuality, adultery, violence, sorcery, and other abominations reach their climax. This "daughter of Babylon" or last Babylon is finally destroyed with the second coming of Christ and his subsequent bowl judgments. (See Isa. 47:5; 48:20; Jer. 50:8, 28; 50:42–46; 51:6, 33, 45; Zech. 2:7–11.)

The Identity of the False Prophet

Revelation 13:11 says the False Prophet will come "out of the earth," implying that he will be a product of the false religious systems of the world. (Conversely, coming "out of the sea" represents the nonreligious aspect of humanity.) It's not hard to imagine then, that the head of the universal religious system of the end times is the counterfeit counterpart to the Holy Spirit and the true church of the Lord Jesus.

Revelation 17:9 tells us the end-times universal religious system will have its headquarters in an area surrounded by "seven hills," speculated to be Rome, including the headquarters of the Roman Catholic Church, the Vatican. The Catholic Church has the most money and influence worldwide of all the religions of the world. The prominent symbolic colors used by the Roman Catholic Church match the "purple and scarlet" in Revelation 17:4.

Rome is inferred to be "Babylon" in 1 Peter 5:13, and the historic record of the early church supports the fact that Rome was often given the code name Babylon. It would therefore be most logical that Rome and the Roman Catholic Church should be central to the sixth world kingdom of Revelation 17:10. (See verses 9b–11 for a discussion on the world kingdoms.) Also, note verse 18: "The woman you saw is the great city that rules over the kings of the earth." We must also remember the vision of the Beast in Daniel 2 describes the strong loins of iron, representing the original Roman Empire, and there now remains for the feet made of iron and clay to rule the earth (Dan. 2:39–43). This revised Roman Empire will be weak, possibly because of the mixture of the political state of Rome with the religious controls of the universal religious system.

If this theory is correct—that the Roman Catholic Church will be central to this future universal religious system—then the False Prophet is most likely the pope, the head of the Roman Catholic Church. The pope is already identified by most individuals and governments as the most important representative of the world church, so the paradigm is already established. Interestingly, the word *catholic* means "universal."

It's interesting to note that Pope Benedict XVI is German born and had an affiliation to Hitler's youth organization. One of the pope's primary goals is to strengthen the church in Europe and bring the religions of the world to greater harmony. Time will determine just what the pope's role will be in end-times events, as well as the identity of the False Prophet.

The "Powers" of the False Prophet

Revelation 13:11 tells us the False Prophet "had two horns like a lamb, but spoke like a dragon." Horns represent power and authority, and the two areas the False Prophet will control are religion and economics.

The False Prophet will mimic Christ in the "lamb" imagery, but he is a wolf in sheep's clothing. He is also Satan's mimic of the Holy Spirit, who draws individuals to Christ (see 1 John 4:2). But the False Prophet will draw people to Satan (Rev. 13:12).

The False Prophet also will have the ability to give life to an image of the Beast and to force people to worship it or face death. So the dragon (Satan), Antichrist, and False Prophet together are a mockery of the Holy Trinity: God the Father, Jesus Christ, and the Holy Spirit.

The False Prophet will be given supernatural powers to deceive the inhabitants of the earth by performing "great and miraculous signs" and "causing fire to come down from heaven" (Rev. 13:13). His powers are similar to those of the "two witnesses," which is not surprising, since the forces of evil love to imitate the powers of righteousness. So if the False Prophet is the pope, a Gentile, and the Antichrist a Jew, then it's likely that their godly counterparts, the two witnesses, will reflect the same heritage. I believe one will be a Jew (Elijah) and the other a Gentile (Enoch). The False Prophet and Antichrist will also be a mockery of the two witnesses, who will be a witness for Christ. (See chapter 20, "The Two Witnesses.")

Sometime around the middle of the tribulation, the False Prophet will cause all unbelievers to take the mark of the Beast, which will give the Antichrist and the False Prophet complete economic and monetary control of the world. Nobody will be able to buy or sell without the mark (Rev. 13:14–18). The Bible says the mark is the number "666," which could be literal or symbolic for the number six, representing the number for humanity or the number of incompletion. This "mark" may be a computer chip under the skin, which will work like a debit card does now, charging a person's bank account for the purchase of goods and services.

The world certainly goes from bad to worse as the tribulation unfolds. Idol worship is magnified, but it is nothing compared to what happens after the "abomination of desolation" and thereafter. The worship of the Antichrist and the "image of the beast" culminates in a degree of satanic worship that the world has never experienced before. (See Dan. 8:10–12; 9:27; 11:36–38; 2 Tim. 3:1–5; 4:3–4; 1 John 2:18–19; Rev. 13:4–8.) The good news is that Christians won't have to hold on much longer. No matter how rough the situation appears, there is hope. Jesus' return will not be far off at this point, and he will come to rescue his children, taking them to spend eternity in glory with him.

Chapter 20

The "two witnesses" (Rev. 11) will play a vital role in God's plan for the end times. Verses 3, 5–6 of Revelation 11 tell us what they'll do:

> And I will give power to my two witnesses, and they will prophesy for 1,260 days, clothed in sackcloth. . . . If anyone tries to harm them, fire comes from their mouths and devours their enemies. This is how anyone who wants to harm them must die. These men have power to shut up the sky so that it will not rain during the time they are prophesying; and they have power to turn the waters into blood and to strike the earth with every kind of plague as often as they want.

As mentioned in the previous chapter, I firmly believe the two witnesses are Enoch and Elijah. The whole crux of the matter revolves around Hebrews 9:27, which states, "Man is destined to die once, and after that to face judgment." The only two men who never faced death were Enoch (see Gen. 5:24) and Elijah (see 2 Kings 2:11). Scripture would be contradicting itself if these two men never died physically. Now, some may say this verse in Hebrews is already contradicted by Lazarus, the ruler's daughter, and many others who were raised from the dead and thus died more than once. Jesus, however, said these individuals were "asleep," as opposed to being dead (Matt. 9:24; 11:11).

They may have been dead by human standards, but not by God's; their spiritual bodies had not separated from their physical bodies. The only exception to Christians facing death is those who will be alive at the time of the rapture. Hebrews 9:28 says, "so Christ was sacrificed once to take away the sins of many people; and he will appear a second time, not to bear sin, but to bring salvation to those who are waiting for him."

Let's look specifically now at Elijah and Enoch.

Evidence of Their Identities

Elijah

For support on Elijah being one of the two witnesses, look at the following verses:

- First Kings 18:38 makes mention of Elijah bringing "fire from heaven."
- James 5:17 says Elijah held rain from the earth.
- Second Kings 2:11 notes that Elijah went straight up to heaven without dying.
- Malachi 4:5 says, "See, I will send you the prophet Elijah before that great and dreadful day of the LORD comes."

Enoch

Support for Enoch being one of the "two witnesses" is found in Jude 14–15: "Enoch, the seventh from Adam, prophesied about these men: 'See, the Lord is coming with thousands upon thousands of his holy ones to judge everyone, and to convict all the ungodly of all the ungodly acts they have done in the ungodly way, and of all the harsh words ungodly sinners have spoken against him.'" This passage suggests that Enoch will prophesy these same words during the tribulation, warning the world of Jesus' coming to judge the world.

Other Clues in Scripture

Other clues to the identities of the two witnesses are found in Revelation 11:3–4 and Zechariah 4:1–14.

In Revelation 11, these men are referred to as "two olive trees" and "two lampstands," lampstands symbolizing churches (Rev. 1:20). Though all seven churches will have representation within the tribulation, only two churches will be true lights for Christ during that time, as the two lampstands represent: the churches of Philadelphia and Smyrna. (See chapter 3.) There are Jewish contingents within these two churches in the last days who will be persecuted by other non-elect Jews. (See Rev. 2:7; 3:7.)

Zechariah 4 also refers to the two witnesses being "two olive trees," but there is only one lampstand instead of two, because this prophecy had a direct implication for the nation Israel, which was a single unified witness for God prior to the age of the Gentile churches. Though the Old Testament saints were not directly referred to as the "church," certainly they are part of the "bride" and members of "one body." Thus they have similar symbolic representation here. (See Isa. 49:18b; Joel 2:16b; Ezek. 16:32; Eph. 3:6; Gal. 3:28; 1 Cor. 12:13.)

The immediate prediction and later fulfillment of Zechariah's prophecy was that Zerubbabel and Joshua the priest, the "two olive trees," would complete the rebuilding of the Jewish temple despite extreme adversity. Verse 14, though, refers to the end-times culmination of the prophecy, where the two witnesses are those who "serve the Lord of all the earth" during the tribulation. Zechariah 4:6 states, "This is the word of the LORD to Zerubbabel: 'Not by might nor by power, but by my Spirit,' says the LORD Almighty." Here Zerubbabel symbolizes the Gentile church age, in which the Holy Spirit permanently indwells believers as the New Testament witness for God. The other "olive tree" directly refers to Joshua the priest, who represents the Jewish church of the Old Testament, where the old-covenant sacrificial system was in place. Both were lights of God and his kingdom throughout history, and both will be lights for Christ during the tribulation.

With Enoch (a Gentile) and Elijah (a Jew) named as the two witnesses in Revelation, this matches up perfectly with the symbolism of the Jewish and Gentile witnesses for Christ during the tribulation and gives further support to the rapture not occurring until the second coming of Christ near the end of the tribulation.

Their Fate

Now that we know the task and the identity of the two witnesses, let's see what happens when their testimony is finished.

> Now when they have finished their testimony, the beast that comes up from the Abyss will attack them, and overpower and kill them. Their bodies will lie in the street of the great city, which is figuratively called Sodom and Egypt, where also their Lord was crucified. For three and a half days men from every people, tribe, language and nation will gaze on their bodies and refuse them burial. The inhabitants of the earth will gloat over them and will celebrate by sending each other gifts, because these two prophets had tormented those who live on the earth.
>
> But after the three and a half days a breath of life from God entered them, and they stood on their feet, and terror struck those who saw them. Then they heard a loud voice from heaven saying to them, "Come up here." And they went up to heaven in a cloud while their enemies looked on.
>
> At that very hour there was a severe earthquake and a tenth of the city collapsed. Seven thousand people were killed in the earthquake, and the survivors were terrified and gave glory to the God of heaven.
>
> The second woe has passed; the third woe is coming soon.
>
> —Rev. 11:7–14

So the Antichrist kills the two witnesses, and the "earth dwellers" are so happy, they send each other gifts to celebrate! But God is not finished with his witnesses. He brings them back to life, and then calls them up to heaven. Immediately, there is a major earthquake that devastates the city and kills thousands. Notice the phrase "at that very hour," which is the literal hour of the sixth trumpet judgment and the subject of the next chapter.

Chapter 21

The vision of the trumpet judgments starts in Revelation 8:2 with a simple introduction: "And I saw the seven angels who stand before God, and to them were given seven trumpets." What gets confusing about this chapter is that John then "fast forwards" in verses 3–5 to a discussion of the bowl judgments before he continues with the details of the individual trumpet judgments. Also, note that the word *then* (Rev. 8:6) is not used in the Greek, because the trumpet judgments do not occur after the seventh seal nor after the bowl judgments, but before them. We'll talk more about the bowl judgments in the following chapter, so for now, let's focus on the remainder of Revelation 8 and 9.

The First Four Trumpets

The first four trumpet judgments focus primarily on God's judgment and wrath against the unrighteous "earth dwellers" and describe physical consequences for humanity's sin.

The First Trumpet

"Then the seven angels who had the seven trumpets prepared to sound them. The first angel sounded his trumpet, and there came hail and fire mixed with blood, and it was hurled down upon the earth. A third of the earth was burned up, a third of the trees were burned up, and all the green grass was burned up" (Rev. 8:6–7). Think of the domino effect of this judgment. With a third of the earth and trees gone and all the green grass, the ratio of carbon dioxide to oxygen will likely be disturbed, affecting the quality of breathable air. The secondary impact on the world's ecosystems will result in the reduction in farmland and grazing areas that will enhance the famine of the third seal.

The Second Trumpet

The second trumpet is described in verses 8–9: "The second angel sounded his trumpet, and something like a huge mountain, all ablaze, was thrown into the sea. A third of the sea turned into blood, a third of the living creatures in the sea died, and a third of the ships were destroyed." It's hard to imagine what devastation this will cause in terms of loss of life, as well as its effect on the world economy, with the loss of the ships and subsequent negative impact on world trade.

The "huge mountain, all ablaze" could be a meteorite, or even something created by God for the sole purpose of carrying out this destructive wrath. In the early part of the tribulation, there will be wars and rumors of wars as the Antichrist is gaining world control, so perhaps this show of God's wrath will be explained away as the result of war or some cosmic disturbance that causes the oceans to turn color. The unsaved world will definitely not see this as a judgment of God. Ironically, though these trumpet judgments are directed against the ungodly, they may indirectly facilitate the Antichrist's world domination, since he will tend to thrive on world chaos.

The Third Trumpet

Verses 10–11 describe the third trumpet: "The third angel sounded his trumpet, and a great star, blazing like a torch, fell from the sky on a third of the rivers and on the springs of water—the name of the star is Wormwood. A third of the waters turned bitter, and many people died from the waters that had become bitter."

Several varieties of bitter-tasting plants in Palestine were used by people of John's time that could be related to the term *wormwood*. Some were used to protect against madness or insanity. This could be a way God shows humanity that they need something to alleviate their "madness," which is what rejection of Christ could be considered. As in the previous trumpet judgment, unsaved people will not see this as coming from God, but will offer other causes, perhaps blaming the pollution of the water on terrorists or nuclear contamination.

The Fourth Trumpet

The fourth trumpet is explained in verse 12: "The fourth angel sounded his trumpet, and a third of the sun was struck, a third of the moon, and a third of the stars, so that a third of them turned dark. A third of the day was without light, and also a third of the night." This is the most difficult of the trumpets to identify, since there are no specifics given as to what will cause this darkness. It does appear that there is total darkness for a third of the time that the heavenly lights are shining in the sky. Could there be some "cloud of darkness" that rotates over the face of the entire earth? Is this from a cosmic or nuclear holocaust, or is this a God-designed sign that tells people they are living in spiritual darkness subsequent to the "abomination of desolation" and the establishment of Antichrist's kingdom of darkness?

Administrators of the First Four Trumpets

The four angels of the first four trumpet judgments are the same angels referenced in Revelation 7:1–3:

> After this I saw four angels standing at the four corners of the earth, holding back the four winds of the earth to prevent any wind from blowing on the land or on the sea or on any tree. Then I saw another angel coming up from the east, having the seal of the living God. He called out in a loud voice to the four angels who had been given power to harm the land and the sea: "Do not harm the land or the sea or the trees until we put a seal on the foreheads of the servants of our God."

While "winds" could symbolize forces of judgment, I prefer the literal interpretation, suggesting that the four angels have control over actual air currents in directing God's wrath over one third of the earth. This would enable these angels of judgment to keep those with the "seal of the living God" from being subjected to the tribulation wrath of God associated with these trumpet judgments. The trees and grass burned up with the first trumpet would be assisted and directed by these winds, and the big waves created by the fall of the "huge mountain all ablaze" could likewise be directed by these winds to target specific ships at sea.

As a side note, the "angel coming up from the east" in verse 2 is most consistent with the archangel Michael, the protector of God's people. Some postulate this to be Jesus, but the statement "servants of our God" instead of "my servants" makes this less likely.

Timing

The fact that the great multitude, including the 144,000 Jewish evangelists, is protected with the "seal of the living God" (see chapter 2) before the land, trees, and sea are afflicted by God's judgment puts the first three trumpet judgments within the first half of the tribulation. Since the fourth trumpet describes darkness analogous to the great spiritual darkness that will come over the earth after the middle of the tribulation when the Antichrist gets ultimate power, it makes sense that this trumpet would start at about the same time. Also occurring at this time is the fourth seal, the pale horse of the apocalypse.

The Last Three Trumpets

The last three trumpets are in a separate class, since they appear to be more demonic and more severe in nature and are prefaced with the statement found in Revelation 8:13: "As I watched, I heard an eagle that was flying in midair call out in a loud voice: 'Woe! Woe! Woe to the inhabitants of the earth, because of the trumpet blasts about to be sounded by the other three angels!'" The "eagle" flying could be an actual eagle or it could represent an angel proclaiming the message of God (Rev. 14:6–10).

The Fifth Trumpet

The fifth trumpet is presented in Revelation 9:1–6:

> The fifth angel sounded his trumpet, and I saw a star that had fallen from the sky to the earth. The star was given the key to the shaft of the Abyss. When he opened the Abyss, smoke rose from it like the smoke from a gigantic furnace. The sun and sky were darkened by the smoke from the Abyss. And out of the smoke locusts came down upon the earth and were given power like that of scorpions of the earth. They were told not to harm the grass of the earth or any plant or tree, but only those people who did not have the seal of God on their foreheads. They were not given power to kill them, but only to torture them for five months. And the agony they suffered was like that of the sting of a scorpion when it strikes a man. During those days men will seek death, but will not find it; they will long to die, but death will elude them.

The "star" that falls is Satan, who loses access to heaven shortly before the middle of the tribulation. The Abyss is the subterranean abode for some of the worst demons. These locust-like demons have a rather grotesque appearance (see Rev. 9:7–10), and they punish the people who do not have the seal of God for five months, which interestingly coincides with the length of time typical locust invasions lasted in biblical times. The leader of these demons is "Abaddon" or "Apollyon," terms for Satan.

It's important to note that the locust-like demons in Revelation 9 are *not* the locusts referred to in Joel 1:2–2:10. The locusts in Joel are God's angels creating the new earth near the end of the tribulation. (More on this in later chapters.) It is interesting how Satan and his demons know Scripture (see James 2:19) and how often they try to mock or imitate God and his forces. The locusts in the Joel prophecy devoured everything in their path, and that is why these demonic locusts likely want to do the same, but are told "not to harm the grass of the earth or any plant or tree, but only those who did not have the seal of God."

The Sixth Trumpet

The sixth trumpet judgment is described in Revelation 9:13–16:

> The sixth angel sounded his trumpet, and I heard a voice coming from the horns of the golden altar that is before God. It said to the sixth angel who had the trumpet, "Release the four angels who are bound at the great river Euphrates." And the four angels who had been kept ready for this very hour and day and month and year were released to kill a third of mankind. The number of the mounted troops was two hundred million. I heard their number.

I believe this sixth trumpet judgment will be very quick, lasting a literal hour on a specific day, in a particular month and year, as the text says. It is worded differently than those verses that refer to figurative hours.

Many preachers in America today proclaim that this 200-million-member army will be an army of humans, probably that of China, which has, in more recent times, boasted an army of this size. However, though the description of these troops (Rev. 9:17–19) could apply to modern-day weapons of destruction, I believe they are demonic forces that are controlled by the four angels currently bound at the Euphrates River. The Greek word used for "riders" here is a neuter form of the word *hippikon*. If they were male humans we would expect a masculine form to be used. We must also remember that the descriptions used for these beings are for the individual troops and *not* weapons of armament. Also, the imagery is grotesque, reminiscent of the locust-like demons controlled by Apollyon in the fifth trumpet judgment. Human soldiers are not typically described as bringing "plagues of fire, smoke and sulfur," yet angels or demons would be capable as agents of such judgment. If this judgment is to occur within a single hour, then 200 million demons could get the job done within this timeframe, but 200 million soldiers would take far longer to accomplish such destruction.

The Seventh Trumpet

Since we've discussed the seventh trumpet at length throughout this book, we won't take the time to do so again here. For review, please see especially Revelation 9–11.

Chapter 22

The "grand finale" of God's tribulation wrath over the world involves the bowl judgments. The bowl judgments last "one hour" in prophetic terms (just over fourteen days), and that is why they are called either "the hour" or "hour of testing" (Rev. 3:10, 11, 13; 14:7; 18:10, 17, 19). Whenever the phrase "peals of thunder, rumblings, flashes of lightning and an earthquake" (Rev. 8:5; 11:19; 16:18) is used, the Bible is referring to the bowl judgments.

Revelation 8:3–5 refers to the bowl judgments as follows:

> Another angel, who had a golden censer, came and stood at the altar. He was given much incense to offer, with the prayers of all the saints, on the golden altar before the throne. The smoke of the incense, together with the prayers of the saints, went up before God from the angel's hand. Then the angel took the censer, filled it with fire from the altar, and hurled it on the earth; and there came peals of thunder, rumblings, flashes of lightning and an earthquake.

The Origin of the Bowls

First mention of the bowl judgments is seen in Revelation 5:8, in which the four living creatures are holding bowls: "Each one had a harp and they were holding golden bowls full of incense, which are the prayers of the saints." The prayers of the saints are valued by God and are often symbolized by incense in Scripture. They are also an offering to God described in Revelation 8:3–5, which was quoted earlier in this chapter. In this scene, the angel with the gold censer is given literal incense that he will offer with the prayers of the saints. Though not specifically mentioned in these verses, I firmly believe that the four living creatures are also present to empty their bowls on the altar. We must remember that the prayers of the saints were stored in those bowls.

So how did the seven angels get the seven bowls? Revelation 15:5–8 (italics added) gives us the answer:

> After this I looked and in heaven the temple, that is, the tabernacle of the Testimony, was opened. Out of the temple came the seven angels with the seven plagues. They were dressed in clean, shining linen and wore golden sashes around their chests. Then one of the four living creatures *gave to the seven angels seven golden bowls* filled with the wrath of God, who lives for ever and ever. And the temple was filled with smoke from the glory of God and from his power, and no one could enter the temple until the seven plagues of the seven angels were completed.

Evidently, after the four living creatures emptied their bowls onto the altar, one of them gave the bowls filled with the wrath of God to the seven angels to release. We should also notice that the mention of the tabernacle opening up is similar to the ark of the covenant opening up in Revelation 11:19, since both are the same event.

The Timing of the Bowl Judgments

The timing of the seven bowl judgments is discussed in Revelation 15:5–8 immediately following the description of the raptured saints standing by the "sea of glass mixed with fire" (Rev. 15:1–2), as the earth is being judged by the bowls and has the appearance of such when viewed by the raptured saints in heaven. (See chapter 9.)

In Revelation 11:18 the seventh trumpet and rapture is discussed, followed by the judgment of the saints. Then verse 19 references the bowl judgments: "Then God's temple in heaven was opened, and within his temple was seen the ark of his covenant. And there came flashes of lightning, rumblings, peals of thunder, an earthquake and a great hailstorm."

Revelation 21:9–10 also gives clues to the timing of the bowl judgments:

> One of the seven angels who had the seven bowls full of the seven last plagues came and said to me, "Come, I will show you the bride, the wife of the Lamb." And he carried me away in the Spirit to a mountain great and high, and showed me the Holy City, Jerusalem, coming down out of heaven from God.

Notice that the bowl judgments have not been released at this time (the bowls are still "full"), and the bride of Christ has been raptured and united with Jesus Christ. Jerusalem is set on Mount Zion, where heaven has been brought at the second coming of Christ.

The Seven Bowl Judgments

Now let us look at the individual bowl judgments.

The First Bowl

The first bowl judgment is discussed in Revelation 16:1–2:

> Then I heard a loud voice from the temple saying to the seven angels, "Go, pour out the seven bowls of God's wrath on the earth." The first angel went and poured out his bowl on the land, and ugly and painful sores broke out on the people who had the mark of the beast and worshiped his image.

The "painful sores" may be reminiscent of the plague of boils experienced by the Egyptians (Ex. 9:8–12). Notice that no mention is made of the saints in this or any of the bowl judgments, because they have already been raptured.

The Second Bowl

The second bowl judgment is referenced in Revelation 16:3, where the sea "turned into blood . . . and every living thing in the sea died." This is similar to the second trumpet judgment, but all of the sea, instead of one third, is affected.

The Third Bowl

The third bowl judgment is likewise similar to the third trumpet, but it affects all the "rivers and springs of water, and they [become] blood" (Rev. 16:4). Blood is so appropriate, as Revelation 16:6 states: "for they have shed the blood of your saints."

The Fourth Bowl

The fourth bowl judgment affects the celestial bodies, as the fourth trumpet, but this judgment increases rather than decreases their intensity. "The sun was given power to scorch people with fire. They were seared by the intense heat and they cursed the name of God, who had control over these plagues, but they refused to repent and glorify him" (Rev. 16:8–9). That is why the bowl judgments are the "hour of testing"—they test unbelievers, showing them they're getting what they deserve, since they refuse to repent and continue the cursing.

The Fifth Bowl

The fifth bowl judgment is cited in Revelation 16:10–11: "The fifth angel poured out his bowl on the throne of the beast, and his kingdom was plunged into darkness. Men gnawed their tongues in agony and cursed the God of heaven because of their pains and their sores, but they refused to repent of what they had done." The darkness here is analogous to the plague of darkness experienced by the Egyptians (Ex. 10:21–29) and corresponds to the spiritual darkness on earth. At this point, the unrepentant "earth dwellers" get a little taste of hell on earth, a prelude to what they will experience for all eternity.

The Sixth and Seventh Bowls

The sixth and seventh bowl judgments have been discussed in great detail in previous chapters, so let me just remind you that the sixth bowl corresponds to the Euphrates River drying up and the forces gathered by demonic coercion for the battle of Armageddon, which then occurs at the seventh bowl judgment.

Chapter 23

The first half of the tribulation will involve "wars and rumors of war" and many natural disasters, famines, and plagues, which sets the stage for the "trinity of evil" to gain its control. The second half of the tribulation, however, will be a time of relative world peace and prosperity for those who are not Christians, including the Jews who did not rebel against the "abomination of desolation." The Babylon of the tribulation starts off with the "great prostitute," the universal religious system, that commits adultery with the kings of the earth as "the inhabitants of the earth were intoxicated with the wine of her adulteries" (Rev. 17:1–2).

Where Is the Last Babylon?

The final or last Babylon starts at the middle of the tribulation, after the Antichrist coordinates the destruction of the prostitute or the universal religious system (Rev. 17:16–18), and causes the "abomination of desolation" (Dan. 9:27). The relative world peace and prosperity created for the unsaved world during the second half of the tribulation is Satan's attempt to mock the upcoming millennial kingdom reign of Christ. Revelation 18:3 states, "For all the nations have drunk the maddening wine of her adulteries. The kings of the earth committed adultery with her, and the merchants of the earth grew rich from her excessive luxuries." The adultery occurs as they indirectly worship Satan and the idols of this world, instead of the only true God.

So the last Babylon is not specifically America or Iraq or any nation for that matter, but all nations that are around during the second half of the tribulation. Zechariah 1:11 says the angels of the Lord search the earth near the second coming and report, "We have gone throughout the earth and found the whole world at rest and in peace." Amos 6:1 states, "Woe to you who are complacent in Zion, and to you who feel secure on Mount Samaria." Even two-thirds of the Jews in Zion will be secure, as they buy the lie of the Antichrist and take the mark of the Beast.

The central headquarters for the last Babylon will be on Mount Samaria, an attempt to mimic Christ's rule adjacent to Mount Zion. (See Jer. 51:25; Hab. 1:6; also chapter 17 for more on this topic.)

Babylon and Tyre

The biblical city of Tyre often symbolizes the last Babylon. Let's examine passages in Ezekiel and Isaiah for more insight into this end-times kingdom.

Ezekiel

Ezekiel 27:1–3 says,

> The word of the LORD came to me: "Son of man, take up a lament concerning Tyre. Say to Tyre, situated at the gateway to the sea, merchant of peoples on many coasts, 'This is what the Sovereign LORD says: "You say, O Tyre, 'I am perfect in beauty.' Your domain was on the high seas; your builders brought your beauty to perfection."'"

So, like Tyre was in those Old Testament days, Babylon will be in the great tribulation. Each will be prosperous and the epitome of luxury and self-indulgence. Both will be controlled by Satan. Both will be successful with world trade and prosperity (Ezek. 27:5–27, 33), but ultimately "The shorelands will quake when your seamen cry out," and "They will weep over you with anguish of soul and with bitter mourning" (Ezek. 27:28, 31). This reference makes analogy to the second coming of Christ and their eventual judgment by God as they both come to ruin.

Ezekiel 28:11–14 gives a detailed description of Satan (represented by the "king of Tyre" in verse 12) in all his beauty as the "anointed guardian cherub," and then verses 16–19 tell what God did to Tyre as a result of its pride:

> Through your widespread trade you were filled with violence, and you sinned. So I drove you in disgrace from the mount of God, and I expelled you, O guardian cherub, from among the fiery stones. Your heart became proud on account of your beauty, and you corrupted your wisdom because of your splendor. So I threw you to the earth; I made a spectacle of you before kings. By your many sins and dishonest trade you have desecrated your sanctuaries. So I made a fire come out from you, and it consumed you, and I reduced you to ashes on the ground in the sight of all who were watching. All the nations who knew you are appalled at you; you have come to a horrible end and will be no more.

Likewise, Satan's same arrogance and pride will cause the last Babylon to be judged.

Isaiah

Isaiah 14:4–7 addresses the fate of the king of Babylon who, like Satan, the king of the last Babylon, will be cut off as follows:

> You will take up this taunt against the king of Babylon: How the oppressor has come to an end! The LORD has broken the rod of the wicked, the scepter of the rulers, which in anger struck down peoples with unceasing blows, and in fury subdued nations with relentless aggression. All the lands are at rest and at peace; they break into singing.

Like the first Babylonian Empire, the last Babylon will be a "relentless aggressor," and the result will be relative world peace and prosperity for those who are its loyalists. The end will come, however, at the appointed time.

Similar analogies between the first and last Babylon are seen in Isaiah 46 and 47, in telescoping prophecies. Referring to the second coming of Christ, Isaiah 46:13 states, "I am bringing my righteousness near, it is not far away; and my salvation will not be delayed. I will grant salvation to Zion, my splendor to Israel." Then, immediately following, Isaiah 47:1–5 states,

> "Go down, sit in the dust, Virgin Daughter of Babylon; sit on the ground without a throne, Daughter of the Babylonians. Take millstones and grind flour; take off your veil. Lift up your skirts, bare your legs, and wade through the streams. Your nakedness will be exposed and your shame uncovered. I will take vengeance; I will spare no one."
>
> Our Redeemer—the LORD Almighty is his name—is the Holy One of Israel.
>
> "Sit in silence, go into darkness, Daughter of the Babylonians; no more will you be called queen of kingdoms."

The "Daughter of the Babylonians" is analogous to the last Babylon (in essence, a final descendant of the first Babylon) that will be judged at the second coming of Christ. (Note also the similar symbolism for religious prostitution between the two Babylons [Rev. 18:3]). This prophecy in Isaiah 47 will be completely fulfilled when all remnants of Babylon are destroyed at the second coming.

Verse 8 specifically refers to the future abominations of the Antichrist and Satan in the last Babylon: "Now then, listen, you wanton creature, lounging in your security and saying to yourself, 'I am, and there is none besides me. I will never be a widow or suffer the loss of children.'"

Notice the mockery of God, who is the "Great I am." Their "lounging" will be over at the appointed time, however. (See also Jer. 51:7–9, 33.)

Isaiah 13:19–20 speaks of the fall of the first and last Babylon, as follows: "Babylon, the jewel of kingdoms, the glory of the Babylonians' pride, will be overthrown by God like Sodom and Gomorrah. She will never be inhabited or lived in through all generations." There will be a new earth at the end of the tribulation, so the last Babylon, unlike the earlier Babylonian Empire, will never be inhabited again. (See also Zech. 2:7–11.)

The heart of end-times prophecy is the nation Israel, and any complete discussion of end-times prophecy should address this nation. In this chapter we'll take a brief look at prophecies that have come to pass in recent years, some of which have been only partially fulfilled, some that will be complete in the millennial kingdom, and others that will be fulfilled when the eternal state is reached. Through it all, we'll see how God cares for and protects his people.

Prophecies Fulfilled

Since the Romans destroyed the Jewish temple in A.D. 70, the Jews were dispersed throughout the Gentile nations of the world. In 1948, however, Israel became a nation—in one day, as prophesied in Isaiah 66:8: "Who has ever heard of such a thing? Who has ever seen such things? Can a country be born in a day, or a nation brought up in a moment?" Since that day, many prophecies have continued to be fulfilled at an accelerated rate.

As prophesied in Isaiah 11:11–12; 43:5–6, 21; and Psalm 107:2–3 immigrants came from the east (Iraq), west (Germany), north (Russia), and lastly from the South (Ethiopia). This prophecy was partially fulfilled in 1990, but it may also be a telescoping prophecy for the return of the messianic Jews during the ingathering at the end of the tribulation.

As prophesied in Ezekiel 37:15–23, Israel was conquered in A.D. 70 as a "divided nation," with a northern and southern kingdom, but the restoration was under "one stick" or "one nation."

As prophesied in Zephaniah 3:8–10 (KJV), Hebrew would once again be the official language of Israel. There is, however, some disagreement among scholars as to the meaning of a "pure" language—whether it is Hebrew or the speech of a converted people, which will definitely be fulfilled within the millennial kingdom.

As prophesied in Ezekiel 45:12–16 and Amos 8:5, the shekel is once again the official currency of Israel.

As prophesied in Isaiah 26:6; 35:1–2; and 41:19, the wilderness surrounding Jerusalem that was once a barren wasteland is now filled with multiple different species of trees.

As prophesied in Amos 9:13, continuous crop rotation has occurred. Since 1948 rainfall has increased 200 percent in Israel, and they have implemented the best irrigation systems in the world. The ultimate fulfillment of this prophecy, however, will take place in the millennium kingdom, when this type of farming efficiency will be seen throughout the whole world.

As prophesied in Ezekiel 36:11, 24, Israel's cities have been renamed to their original names: Jerusalem, Nazareth, Bethlehem, and Beersheba, for example.

As prophesied in Jeremiah 32:44, prosperity has increased in the area.

As prophesied in Hosea 3:4–5, a form of government other than a monarchy has been established.

As prophesied in Zechariah 12:3, Israel has become a hotbed of international and political turmoil.

As prophesied in Ezekiel 39:17, the valley of Jezreel or Megiddo, where the battle of Armageddon is to occur, has seen a great increase in the vulture population, setting the stage for the "great feast."

As prophesied in Ezekiel 44:1–2, the east gate is to be closed prior to the second coming of Christ. A cemetery has been built there. The area is now owned by Muslims who know the prophecy about the second coming, and they believe no "high priest" like Jesus will go through a cemetery. But they don't realize that Jesus will actually move the cemetery with an earthquake at his second coming. (See Zech. 14:4.)

The Fig Tree

One of the most quoted end-times prophecies about Israel involves the "fig tree" analogy, as we discussed briefly in the introduction. The fig tree is mentioned multiple times in the Bible, and clearly represents the nation Israel. (See Jer. 24:5; Joel 1:7.) Jesus said,

> Now learn this lesson from the fig tree: As soon as its twigs get tender and its leaves come out, you know that summer is near. Even so, when you see all these things, you know that it is near, right at the door. I tell you the truth, this generation will certainly not pass away until all these things have happened. Heaven and earth will pass away, but my words will never pass away.
> —Matt. 24:32–35

The fig tree produces fruit in two cycles. The first crop is in late June, which would be analogous to the 144,000 Jewish evangelists coming to Christ and the Jews who are converted through their witness. The second crop of fruit occurs in early September and would correspond to the large-scale Jewish conversion that will occur after the second coming of Christ. (More on this in the next chapter.) Since both crops occur in the same year, it's not unreasonable to conclude that the rapture and the final ingathering of the harvest would also occur in the same year or season. Conversely, a pretribulation rapture would be analogous to a fig yielding its first fruits seven years prior to yielding its final fruits. Likewise, in the Jewish festival seasons, the celebration of the "firstfruits" and the "ingathering" occur in the same year. (See Ex. 23:16; 34:22; Num. 28:28; Lev. 23:9–14.)

Taking the fig tree analogy a step further, we see that the typical span between the first and second harvests is seventy-five days—the same time that will elapse between the rapture and the start of the millennial kingdom (after the ingathering of the Jews). Isn't that fascinating?

In Matthew 24, Jesus said "this generation"—the one that sees the "leaves come out"—will live to see the culmination of the end-times prophecies. Israel became a nation in 1948 and has indeed grown and prospered; most scholars would agree that the green leaves have grown out. A generation lasts anywhere from forty to eighty years, depending on which Bible scholar you talk to. (See Ps. 90:10.) So, if we take a conservative estimate that the "green shoots" of the fig tree developed for Israel within twenty years after it became a nation in 1948, and add forty to eighty years to that date, then we would estimate that the culmination of the end times could very well be reached any time between 2008 and 2048. We are indeed in the last days if we have the timing of this prophecy right.

The Jewish Church

Though many biblical prophecies for unrepentant Israel have been fulfilled, the Jewish church timeline has been put on hold since the Jews rejected Christ at his first coming and crucified him. This is affirmed in the prophecy of the "seventy sevens" in Daniel 9:25–26:

> Know and understand this: From the issuing of the decree to restore and rebuild Jerusalem until the Anointed One, the ruler, comes, there will be seven "sevens," and sixty-two "sevens." It will be rebuilt with streets and a trench, but in times of trouble. After the sixty-two "sevens," the Anointed One will be cut off.

It took forty-nine years, or "seven sevens" from the decree that King Artaxerxes issued to rebuild the wall around Jerusalem. It then took 434 years, or sixty-two "sevens," from the wall being rebuilt until Christ was crucified on the cross. There is only "one seven" left in Jewish church history. The "age of the Gentiles" started at Pentecost. The last seven years of Jewish church history will start during the tribulation and last to the end of this age. Gentile church history ends at the rapture. Of course, though we may compartmentalize church history in a Jewish or Gentile church, we must realize that the true church incorporates both Jews and Gentiles, and we are all in one body, with Christ as its head.

What is next for Israel prior to the start of the tribulation is open to some speculation. There should be some sort of crisis brewing for Israel, because the world's hatred for the Jewish people will have them on the brink of extinction when the tribulation starts. As postulated previously, I feel America will fall as a world superpower, which will have a serious, destabilizing effect on Israel. Fortunately for Israel, the Antichrist will create a peace treaty at the start of the tribulation, but this will be only a temporary solution to their problem. There will initially be "good times" for Israel after the peace treaty is signed and within the first three-and-a-half years of the tribulation, during which time the Jewish temple will be rebuilt.

Since the Jewish temple was overthrown in A.D. 70, all the records of those who were descendents of the Levite priests were lost. But in July of 1998, a gene marker was identified on the Y-chromosome, whereby all Levite ancestors can now potentially be identified. The "ashes of the red heifer" (Num. 19) are also required for temple worship to resume. Unfortunately, the ashes were also lost when the temple was destroyed. Even more challenging, the red heifer is a rare genetic mutation that takes two thousand years or so to naturally occur. Amazingly, in May 1997, a red heifer was identified in America, so the ashes are now available. Additionally, most of the musical instruments used in the temple worship have again been recreated. So, as you can see, once the Antichrist establishes a peace treaty, the prerequisites for reinstitution of temple worship will have been met. According to tradition, temple sacrifices will begin again once the cornerstone of the temple is laid.

The Place of Refuge

At the mid-point of tribulation the "abomination of desolation" will occur when the Antichrist will enter the temple and defile it. Then he will stop all religious activity except the worship of him. At this time, God will direct the Jewish people to leave Jerusalem:

> Then let those who are in Judea flee to the mountains. Let no one on the roof of his house go down to take anything out of the house. Let no one in the field go back to get his cloak. How dreadful it will be in those

days for pregnant women and nursing mothers! Pray
that your flight will not take place in winter or on the
Sabbath. For then there will be great distress, unequaled
from the beginning of the world until now—and never
to be equaled again.
—Matt. 24:16–21 (see also Mark 12:14–19)

Petra and Bozrah are the most common names given to the place of
refuge God will provide for those who heed his warning, though it is
also called Sela, Mount Hor, Rock City of the Edomites or Remnant
of Edom, and Mount Seir. It is here that they will be protected by
God for three and a half years. This place of refuge is a ghost town
about 120 miles southeast of Jerusalem, located in a rugged mountain
wilderness area surrounded by desert in modern-day southern Jordan.
Petra overlooks the Valley of Jezreel, where the battle of Armageddon is
to take place. It has the capability of housing one million people, which
is around one-third the size of the nation Israel at this time. (For other
references to the place of refuge, see Ps. 108:10; Ezek. 19:10–15; Hos.
2:14; Mic. 2:12; Zeph. 2:1; Rev. 12:6, 14–16; and see Ex. 19:4; Deut.
32:9–12 for "eagle's wings" protecting Israel.)

Now let's look at a few verses addressing God's protection of the remnant of Israel at Bozrah through "Jacob's trouble" and the associated
cataclysmic events of the seven bowl judgments that will be occurring
around them.

Isaiah 26:20–21 says,

Go, my people, enter your rooms and shut the doors
behind you; hide yourselves for a little while until his
wrath has passed by. See, the LORD is coming out of
his dwelling to punish the people of the earth for their
sins. The earth will disclose the blood shed upon her;
she will conceal her slain no longer.

So, by this time either the doors have been built to the rooms of the
ruins at Bozrah or God supernaturally provides such doors to protect
them from his second-coming wrath, or this reference could be totally

symbolic. This is analogous to the death angel passing by the Israelites in Egypt because of the blood on their doorposts. (See Ex. 11.)

Zephaniah 1:14–2:3 talks of the Jews being gathered together to avoid the second-coming wrath of God.

Psalm 57:1 states, "I will take refuge in the shadow of your wings until the disaster has passed."

Refined "Like Silver"

One-third of the Jews who experience the tribulation will be refined through it and eventually saved. Zechariah 13:8–9 says,

> "In the whole land," declares the LORD, "two-thirds will be struck down and perish; yet one-third will be left in it. This third I will bring into the fire; I will refine them like silver and test them like gold. They will call on my name and I will answer them; I will say, 'They are my people,' and they will say, 'The LORD is our God.'"

So those of Israel who do not flee to the mountains at the time of the abomination of desolation will go through intense persecution for the second half of the tribulation, and will encounter the harshest judgment from God, which is called "Jacob's trouble." Jeremiah 30:7 says, "How awful that day will be! None will be like it. It will be a time of trouble for Jacob, but he will be saved out of it." The Hebrew word used for "saved out" more closely means "saved through." So Israel will go through "Jacob's trouble."

Though Israel is severely punished by God around the time of the second coming, the remnant is still saved. Jeremiah 30:11 states, "'I am with you and will save you,' declares the LORD. 'Though I completely destroy all the nations among which I scatter you, I will not completely destroy you. I will discipline you but only with justice; I will not let you go entirely unpunished.'" God will "destroy the nations" with the "final hour" of judgment and the battle of Armageddon, but he will eventually save most of Israel, those who are still alive near the end of the tribulation.

The Jews who stay in Jerusalem after the abomination of desolation and become Christians before the great revival are the exceptions to the rule. These Jews, though they get saved early, suffer far more through Jacob's Trouble than those at Bozrah. Those remaining in Israel after the abomination of desolation, as well as those scattered throughout the world and remaining in the last Babylon, represent the Jewish component of the church of Smyrna, since they eventually incur the harshest persecution. Jesus addressed this group prophetically:

> Be on your guard against men; they will hand you over to the local councils and flog you in their synagogues. On my account you will be brought before governors and kings as witnesses to them and to the Gentiles. But when they arrest you, do not worry about what to say or how to say it. At that time you will be given what to say, for it will not be you speaking, but the Spirit of your Father speaking through you.

> Brother will betray brother to death, and a father his child; children will rebel against their parents and have them put to death. All men will hate you because of me, but he who stands firm to the end will be saved. When you are persecuted in one place, flee to another. I tell you the truth, you will not finish going through the cities of Israel before the Son of Man comes.
>
> —Matt. 10:17–23

These messianic Jews are the ones being turned over to the authorities by their fellow Jews for refusing to worship the Beast. They are definitely "saved" at this point, since the text says they are "witnesses," and the "Spirit" within them gives them the words to say to their accusers. They will flee from one city to another within Israel, trying to avoid capture. Some of these messianic Jews are martyred for their faith, and the rest are raptured at the second coming of Christ.

There are many other verses that reference the severe persecution faced by those Jews who don't flee at the "abomination of desolation" and the last Babylon.

Zechariah 14:1–2 states, "A day of the LORD is coming when your plunder will be divided among you. I will gather all the nations to Jerusalem to fight against it; the city will be captured, the houses ransacked, and the women raped. Half of the city will go into exile, but the rest of the people will not be taken away." Here the evil Jews will be purged from Jerusalem, and the pure remnant will remain in the city Jerusalem. Many of the true remnant in Israel will be in jail or in hiding at the time of the final assault, so hopefully they will be spared some of the torture that the unsaved Jews will suffer. There will also be some elect Jews who have not converted to Christ yet who will remain in the city even after the assault. It's important to remember that there is still a Jewish remnant in Bozrah, and that there are still Jews scattered throughout the world who are still part of the remnant.

Zechariah 12:2–3 states, "I am going to make Jerusalem a cup that sends all the surrounding peoples reeling. Judah will be besieged as well as Jerusalem. On the day, when all the nations of the earth are gathered against her, I will make Jerusalem an immovable rock for all the nations." Jerusalem is devastated after an initial assault by many of the same armies that are involved in the later battle of Armageddon. Though it is besieged, however, the city is purified through it. (See Zech. 14:1–16.)

Ezekiel 20:38 also references the cleansing of Jerusalem: "I will purge you of those who revolt and rebel against me. I will bring them out of the land where they are living, yet they will not enter the land of Israel. Then you will know that I am the LORD." Those who cannot return to Israel are those who have taken the side of the Antichrist.

Isaiah 4:1, 4 states, "In that day seven women will take hold of one man and say, 'We will eat our own food and provide our own clothes; only let us be called by your name. Take away our disgrace!' . . . The Lord will wash away the filth of the women of Zion; he will cleanse the blood-stains from Jerusalem by a spirit of judgment and a spirit of fire."

Amos 5:3 makes reference to only 10 percent of the fighting troops of Israel being left after the last assault on the city Jerusalem.

Ezekiel 38 describes the time of the devastation of Israel near the end, prior to the battle of Armageddon. Israel is attacked by Gog and

Magog, which many believe represent an alliance between Russian and Arab nations. Verses 11–12 say,

> You will say, "I will invade a land of unwalled villages; I will attack a peaceful and unsuspecting people—all of them living without walls and without gates and bars. I will plunder and loot and turn my hand against the resettled ruins and the people gathered from the nations, rich in livestock and goods, living at the center of the land."

Some Bible scholars claim that the battle of Gog and Magog cannot be the battle of Armageddon, because Israel could not be a peaceful and unsuspecting people at that time.

Daniel 11:21 states, "He will be succeeded by a contemptible person who has not been given the honor of royalty. He will invade the kingdom when its people feel secure, and he will seize it through intrigue." (See also Amos 6:1.)

The reality of the matter is that Israel's leadership and socioeconomic structure will be thriving near the end of the tribulation, because those submitting to the Antichrist and those having the "mark of the beast" will be living in peace and prosperity. The Jews who rebel against the Antichrist and who stay within Israel will either be in hiding or in prison.

After an initial victory by the invaders from the north, it appears that Christ rescues those who are left in Israel at his second coming.

Christ's Rescue

After the city of Jerusalem is besieged for the last time, and the remaining Jews are on the verge of extinction, then Christ Jesus will come to their rescue. Zechariah 14:3–5 says,

> Then the LORD will go out and fight against those nations, as he fights in the day of battle. On that day his feet will stand on the Mount of Olives, east of Jerusalem, and the Mount of Olives will be split in two

from east to west, forming a great valley, with half of
the mountain moving north and half moving south.
You will flee by my mountain valley, for it will extend
to Azel. You will flee as you fled from the earthquake in
the days of Uzziah king of Judah. Then the LORD my
God will come, and all the holy ones with him.

Because Azel is near Bozrah, it has been postulated that those Jews
who flee through the great valley created by the second coming of Christ
will unite with the Jews already at Bozrah. Ezekiel 7:15–17 states,

> Outside is the sword, inside are plague and famine;
> those in the country will die by the sword, and those in
> the city will be devoured by famine and plague. All who
> survive and escape will be in the mountains, moaning
> like doves of the valleys, each because of his sins. Every
> hand will go limp, and every knee will become as weak
> as water.

So it appears that some unregenerate but elect Jews remain in Israel
after the purging, but all who remain will eventually be converted
to Christ. Amos 3:11–12 says, "Therefore this is what the Sovereign
LORD says: 'An enemy will overrun the land; he will pull down your
strongholds and plunder your fortresses.' This is what the LORD says:
'As a shepherd saves from the lion's mouth only two leg bones or a
piece of an ear, so will the Israelites be saved.'" Then in Zechariah 3:2
we read, "The LORD said to Satan, 'The LORD, rebuke you, Satan!
The LORD, who has chosen Jerusalem, rebuke you! Is not this man
a burning stick snatched from the fire?'" In this verse Satan himself
is seen as the one trying to exterminate Jerusalem, but the remnant is
pulled out by God as one would pull a burning stick out of the fire just
in time. Our God is an on-time God!

Before the final purging of Jerusalem, God appears to mark the Jews
who are going to be spared the slaughter because they are regenerate or
will later accept Jesus as Lord. In Ezekiel 9:4–6 God says,

> "Go throughout the city of Jerusalem and put a mark on the foreheads of those who grieve and lament over all the detestable things that are done in it."
>
> As I listened, he said to the others, "Follow him through the city and kill, without showing pity or compassion. Slaughter old men, young men and maidens, women and children, but do not touch anyone who has the mark. Begin at my sanctuary." So they began with the elders who were in front of the temple.

Then Isaiah 9:13–14 states: "But the people have not returned to him who struck them, nor have they sought the LORD Almighty. So the LORD will cut off from Israel both head and tail, both palm branch and reed in a single day." Isaiah 10:17–19 states,

> The Light of Israel will become a fire, their Holy One a flame; in a single day it will burn and consume his thorns and his briers. The splendor of his forests and fertile fields it will completely destroy, as when a sick man wastes away. And the remaining trees of his forests will be so few that a child could write them down.

Isaiah 17:4–6 says, "In that day the glory of Jacob will fade; the fat of his body will waste away. It will be as when a reaper gathers the standing grain and harvests the grain with his arm—as when a man gleans heads of grain in the Valley of Rephaim. Yet some gleanings will remain, as when an olive tree is beaten." (See also Ps. 50:7, 15; Isa. 26:18; 54:7; 66:8–9; Jer. 30:7; Ezek. 7:18–19; 38:11; Hos. 13:7–8; Amos 5:18; Mic. 5:3; 7:2; Zeph. 1:7–8, 18; Zech. 13:2; Heb. 10:30; John 16:20.)

Nationwide Repentance

Will Israel finally repent as a nation in the end? Romans 11:25–26 gives us the answer: "Israel has experienced a hardening in part until the full number of the Gentiles has come in. And so all Israel will be saved." Thus, Israel will be saved after the full number of the Gentiles comes to the faith and the church is raptured.

Several other references support widespread repentance.

- "Many will be purified, made spotless and refined, but the wicked will continue to be wicked" (Dan. 12:10).
- "For on my holy mountain, the high mountain of Israel, declares the Sovereign LORD, there in the land the entire house of Israel will serve me, and there I will accept them" (Ezek. 20:40).
- "And I will pour out on the house of David and the inhabitants of Jerusalem a spirit of grace and supplication. They will look on me, the one they have pierced, and they will mourn for him as one mourns for an only child, and grieve bitterly for him as one grieves for a firstborn son" (Zech. 12:10).
- "On that day a fountain will be opened to the house of David and the inhabitants of Jerusalem, to cleanse them from sin and impurity" (Zech. 13:1).
- "'In that day,' declares the LORD, 'you will call me "my husband"; you will no longer call me "my master"'" (Hos. 2:16).
- "For the Israelites will live many days without king or prince, without sacrifice or sacred stones, without ephod or idol. Afterward the Israelites will return and seek the LORD their God and David their king. They will come trembling to the LORD and to his blessings in the last days" (Hos. 3:4–5).
- "In that day the remnant of Israel, the survivors of the house of Jacob, will no longer rely on him who struck them down but will truly rely on the LORD, the Holy One of Israel. A remnant will return, a remnant of Jacob will return to the Mighty God" (Isa. 10:20–21).
- See also Psalm 50:15; Isaiah 17:7; 27:6; 45:17; Jeremiah 30:7; Ezekiel 7:27; 20:38; and Hosea 3:5.

How Many Will Repent?

There is some debate about whether all or only a majority of the remaining Jews will accept Jesus as Lord. I tend to believe that most but not all will convert to Christianity. My reasoning is found in Revelation 3:9, which discusses Jews from the synagogue of Satan bowing at the feet of the converted tribulation Jews, after the end of the tribulation. How can this occur if there are not some Jews who survive the tribulation wrath without repenting? (See also Isa. 66:18.) Also, when the word *all* is used in Scripture, it does not always mean every individual. (See 1 Tim. 4:10.) If all Jews did not believe the gospel message after the first coming of Christ, it seems consistent that not all will believe the message after the second coming. Romans 10:14–15 talks about the "good news" of the gospel message that started after the first coming of Christ, and then verses 16 and 18 state, "But not all the Israelites accepted the good news. For Isaiah says, 'Lord, who has believed our message?' . . . But I ask: Did they not hear? Of course they did: 'Their voice has gone out into all the earth, their words to the ends of the world.'"

When Will It Happen?

So when does Israel acknowledge Jesus as Lord and Savior? Habakkuk 3:12–13 states, "In wrath you strode through the earth and in anger you threshed the nations. You came out to deliver your people." From this reference it's clear that the revival occurs sometime after the second coming of Christ.

In Isaiah 63:1–3 we read,

> Who is this coming from Edom, from Bozrah, with his garments stained crimson? Who is this, robed in splendor, striding forward in the greatness of his strength?
>
> "It is I, speaking in righteousness, mighty to save."
>
> Why are your garments red, like those of one treading the winepress?
>
> "I have trodden the winepress alone; from the nations no one was with me [no one from Israel]. I trampled them in my anger and trod them down in my wrath; their blood spattered my garments."

Evidently, Jesus pays a visit to Israel in Bozrah after Armageddon, and they still don't accept him, so he returns to Mount Zion.

Hosea 5:15–6:2 states,

> Then I will go back to my place [Mount Zion] until they admit their guilt. And they will seek my face; in their misery they will earnestly seek me. Come, let us return to the LORD. He has torn us to pieces but he will heal us; he has injured us but he will bind up our wounds. After two days he will revive us; on the third day he will restore us, that we may live in his presence.

It appears, then, that the nation repents on the third day after Armageddon and Jesus' first visit to Bozrah. Zechariah 3:9 says, "I will remove the sin of this land in a single day." And then in Isaiah 18:3–4 we read, "All you people of the world, you who live on the earth, when a banner is raised on the mountains, you will see it, and when the trumpet sounds you will hear it. This is what the LORD says to me: 'I will remain quiet and will look on from my dwelling place.'" The trumpet call is for the "great ingathering" before the millennial kingdom begins. (See chapter 26.) It appears that after visiting Bozrah, Jesus will return to Mount Zion to wait for Israel's repentance.

Several other scriptures reference the Jewish revival shortly after the battle of Armageddon.

Ezekiel 38–39 details the prophecy against Gog and Magog, with later references to the battle of Armageddon. According to 39:7, the revival of the Jewish people appears to occur after Armageddon, when, God says, "I will make known my holy name among my people Israel."

Zephaniah 3:8–9, 13 states,

> I have decided to assemble the nations, to gather the kingdoms and to pour out my wrath on them—all my fierce anger. The whole world will be consumed by the fire of my jealous anger. Then will I purify the lips of the peoples, that all of them may call on the name of the Lord and serve him shoulder to shoulder. . . . The remnant of Israel will do no wrong.

Isaiah 30:26 says, "The moon will shine like the sun, and the sunlight will be seven times brighter, like the light of seven full days, when the LORD binds up the bruises of his people and heals the wounds he inflicted." The same event appears to be expressed in the fourth bowl judgment in Revelation 16:8, 9–10, where it says the sun will be "given power to scorch people." This combination of verses indicates the repentance of Israel does not occur until sometime after the fourth bowl judgment.

The revival of the nation Israel is described in Ezekiel 37:11–14 in symbolic terms. For example, "dry bones" in the desert come to life after God "breathes on them."

Where Will They Be?

Where are all the Jews located when they are finally saved? Jeremiah 30:10–11 tells us,

> "I will surely save you out of a distant place, your descendants from the land of their exile. Jacob will again have peace and security, and no one will make him afraid. I am with you and will save you," declares the LORD. "Though I completely destroy all the nations among which I scatter you, I will not completely destroy you."

I believe this is referring not only to the Jews in Bozrah, but also to those scattered throughout the world who will ultimately come to a belief in Christ. Zechariah 8:7 says, "This is what the LORD Almighty says: 'I will save my people from the countries of the east and the west.'" And then 10:8–9 says, "I will signal for them and gather them in. Surely I will redeem them; they will be as numerous as before. Though I scatter them among the peoples, yet in distant lands they will remember me. They and their children will survive, and they will return."

Chapter 25

The prophet Joel talks about an outpouring of God's Spirit in the last days on both Jews and Gentiles, so it appears that a great revival occurs after the second coming of Christ and his judgment of the world. In Joel 2:28–32 we read,

> And afterward, I will pour out my Spirit on all people. Your sons and daughters will prophesy, your old men will dream dreams, your young men will see visions. Even on my servants, both men and women, I will pour out my Spirit in those days. I will show wonders in the heavens and on the earth, blood and fire and billows of smoke. The sun will be turned to darkness and the moon to blood before the coming of the great and dreadful day of the LORD. And everyone who calls on the name of the LORD will be saved; for on Mount Zion and in Jerusalem there will be deliverance, as the LORD has said, among the survivors whom the LORD calls.

This passage appears to support both a Gentile and a Jewish revival, near the end of tribulation and after the second coming of Christ, because it talks of God pouring his Spirit out on "all people."

Zechariah 14:16–17 says,

> Then the survivors from all the nations that have at-
> tacked Jerusalem will go up year after year to worship
> the King, the LORD Almighty, and to celebrate the
> Feast of Tabernacles. If any of the peoples of the earth
> do not go up to Jerusalem to worship the King, the
> LORD Almighty, they will have no rain.

Those born again Jews and Gentiles who are part of the end-times revival will remain on the earth in non-glorified bodies during the millennium period, and repopulate the earth through this one-thou-sand-year period. How awesome that God is willing to allow people to be converted at the very end, even those fighting against him at Armageddon. Maybe that is why the place where Armageddon occurs is called the "valley of decision" (Joel 3:14).

Although God judges the earth severely during the tribulation, he still allows a few survivors, as affirmed by Isaiah 24:6: "Therefore earth's inhabitants are burned up and very few are left." These survivors will be a mixture of Jews and Gentiles—some who will eventually convert to Christ and some who will reject him.

The Messengers

During this greatest revival in the history of the world, what are the raptured saints doing? They are blessed to be the messengers bringing the good news! Many references support this idea, so we'll explore just a few.

- "You who bring good tidings to Zion, go up on a high mountain. You who bring good tidings to Jerusalem, lift up your voice with a shout, lift it up, do not be afraid; say to the towns of Judah 'Here is your God!' See, the Sovereign LORD comes with power, and his arm rules for him. See, his reward is with him and his recompense accompanies him" (Isa. 40:9–10).
- "Look, there on the mountains, the feet of one who brings good news, who proclaims peace! Celebrate your festivals, O Judah, and fulfill your vows. No more will the wicked invade you; they will be completely destroyed" (Nah. 1:15).

- "Deliverers will go up on Mount Zion to govern the mountains of Esau. And the kingdom will be the Lord's" (Obad. 21). The Hebrew word for "deliverers" here means to "bring salvation, deliver, preserve, or save." We must remember that the Deliverer is the Lord Jesus Christ (Rom. 11:26), but we go in his name.

- "'Everyone who calls on the name of the Lord will be saved.' How, then, can they call on the one they have not believed in? And how can they believe in the one of whom they have not heard? And how can they hear without someone preaching to them? And how can they preach unless they are sent? As it is written, 'How beautiful are the feet of those who bring good news!' But not all the Israelites accepted the good news. For Isaiah says, 'Lord who has believed our message?' Consequently, faith comes from hearing the message, and the message is heard through the word of Christ. But I ask: Did they not hear? Of course they did: 'Their voice has gone out into all the earth, their words to the ends of the world'" (Rom. 10:13–18; see Isa. 52:7). As the good news went out from Zion to the entire world at the first coming of Christ, likewise the good news at the second coming of Christ will go out to the entire world, but this time to every survivor of the tribulation.

- "So will he sprinkle many nations, and kings will shut their mouths because of him. For what they were not told, they will see, and what they have not heard, they will understand. Who has believed our message and to whom has the arm of the LORD been revealed?" (Isa. 52:15–53:1; see Rom. 15:21).

The Message

In Isaiah 40:28 we read, "Do you not know? Have you not heard? The LORD is the everlasting God, the Creator of the ends of the earth. He will not grow weary, and his understanding no one can fathom." And Isaiah 62:11 says, "The LORD has made proclamation to the ends of the earth: 'Say to the Daughter of Zion, "See, your Savior comes! See, his reward is with him, and his recompense accompanies him."'" I believe the raptured saints will have this same message to the Jews—the

Lord Jesus is the everlasting God who wants to save them, and they can call on him.

Not only will the raptured saints share the gospel with the Jews, but some of the surviving Jews will ask them for directions to Zion: "'In those days, at that time,' declares the LORD, 'the people of Israel and the people of Judah together will go in tears to seek the LORD their God. They will ask the way to Zion and turn their faces toward it. They will come and bind themselves to the LORD in an everlasting covenant that will not be forgotten'" (Jer. 50:4–5).

Jesus said, "And this gospel of the kingdom will be preached in the whole world as a testimony to all nations, and then the end will come" (Matt. 24:14). Many believe that the "whole world" terminology used here is "all people groups" or "all nations." The Greek word *kosmos* used for "whole world" does include the more limited interpretation, but I believe that literally all individuals will have the gospel preached to them, as Christ will be on Mount Zion, clearly seen by all (Rev. 6:16–17).

What an incredible event this will be, and how exciting to know that as believers in Christ, we will be a part of it!

THE GREAT INGATHERING

Chapter 26

The battle of Armageddon and the culmination of the tribulation period are followed by the "ingathering" process, in which all the Jewish and Gentile survivors throughout the world go back to Jerusalem, where Jesus sorts out those who are blessed to enter the millennium kingdom and those who will go to gehenna. According to Daniel 12:12, this process of sorting whereby the tribulation survivors come back to Jerusalem takes around 45 days: "Blessed is the one who waits for and reaches the end of the 1,335 days"—when the millennium starts. Subtract the number of days on the Jewish timeline from the abomination of desolation to the end—1,290—from 1,335 when the millennium starts, and you get 45. So 45 days is the time allotted for the ingathering.

Isaiah 45:20–25 gives this description of the event:

> Gather together and come; assemble, you fugitives from the nations. Ignorant are those who carry about idols of wood, who pray to gods that cannot save. Declare what is to be, present it—let them take counsel together. Who foretold this long ago, who declared it from the distant past? Was it not I, the LORD? And there is no God apart from me, a righteous God and a Savior; there is none but me.
>
> Turn to me and be saved, all you ends of the earth; for I am God, and there is no other. By myself I have sworn,

my mouth has uttered in all integrity a word that will not be revoked: Before me every knee will bow; by me every tongue will swear. They will say of me, "In the LORD alone are righteousness and strength." All who have raged against him will come to him and be put to shame. But in the LORD all the descendants of Israel will be found righteous and will exult.

In this chapter we'll look at how the Bible describes the great ingathering, and how the two groups of survivors—believers and unbelievers—will respond.

Biblical Illustrations of the Ingathering

In Jesus' well-known illustration of the sheep and the goats, he made clear the eternal destinations of both groups.

When the Son of Man comes in his glory, and all the angels with him, he will sit on his throne in heavenly glory. All the nations will be gathered before him, and he will separate the people one from another as a shepherd separates the sheep from the goats. He will put the sheep on his right and the goats on his left.

Then the King will say to those on his right, "Come, you who are blessed by my Father; take your inheritance, the kingdom prepared for you since the creation of the world." . . .

Then he will say to those on his left, "Depart from me, you who are cursed, into the eternal fire prepared for the devil and his angels." . . .

Then they will go away to eternal punishment, but the righteous to eternal life.

—Matt. 25:31–34, 41, 46

Those Christians who enter the millennial kingdom are promised "eternal life" at the end of the millennium, and they will never die. It's only their unsaved progeny who could possibly die during the millennial period.

Isaiah 24:21–23 says,

> In that day the LORD will punish the powers in
> the heavens above and the kings on the earth below.
> They will be herded together like prisoners bound
> in a dungeon; they will be shut up in prison and be
> punished after many days. The moon will be abashed,
> the sun ashamed; for the LORD Almighty will reign
> on Mount Zion and in Jerusalem, and before its elders,
> gloriously.

The saved will be allowed into the millennium kingdom, where the sun and moon will have insignificant glory compared to the radiance of the Lord and his saints.

Ezekiel 34:17 states, "As for you, my flock, this is what the Sovereign LORD says: I will judge between one sheep and another, and between rams and goats."

Unbelieving Survivors

Tragically some survivors of the tribulation will come before the Lord having not trusted him for salvation. They will have had their last chance to call on the name of the Lord at the end of the tribulation when they saw Jesus coming to Mount Zion and heard the witness of the raptured saints throughout the earth. But once the tribulation is over and the ingathering process is started, it will be too late. Many will bow and confess, but to no avail. (See Matt. 7:21–23.)

It appears that there is a role reversal during the "ingathering" process, where the fugitives for Christ become the captors. Two passages in Isaiah shed light on this phenomenon.

> The LORD will have compassion on Jacob; once again
> he will choose Israel and will settle them in their own
> land. Aliens will join them and unite with the house of
> Jacob. Nations will take them and bring them to their

own place. And the house of Israel will possess the nations as menservants and maidservants in the LORD's land. They will make captives of their captors and rule over their oppressors.

—Isa. 14:1–2

. . . they will trudge behind you, coming over to you in chains. They will bow down before you and plead with you, saying, "Surely God is with you and there is no other; there is no other god."

"Truly you are a God who hides himself, O God and Savior of Israel. All the makers of idols will be put to shame and disgraced; they will go off into disgrace together. But Israel will be saved by the LORD with an everlasting salvation; you will never be put to shame or disgraced, to ages everlasting" (Isa. 45:15–17).

So these unsaved survivors will bow before the saved Jews scattered among the nations at the end of the tribulation. They will recognize God and his Spirit in other Christians, but it will be too late. They will claim that God "hides himself," attempting to rationalize their ignorance, and plead with Christians and God himself, but it will be too late.

Once the tribulation comes to a close, the whole world will know the truth, and those who aren't truly born again will have a sense of urgency to return to Jerusalem. They will try to be identified with and travel with the people of God, but, again, it will be too late. Zechariah 8:20–23 states,

This is what the LORD Almighty says: "Many peoples and the inhabitants of many cities will yet come, and the inhabitants of one city will go to another and say, 'Let us go at once to entreat the LORD and seek the LORD Almighty. I myself am going.' And many peoples and powerful nations will come to Jerusalem to seek the LORD Almighty and to entreat him."

> This is what the LORD Almighty says: "In those days ten men from all languages and nations will take firm hold of one Jew by the hem of his robe and say, 'Let us go with you, because we have heard that God is with you.'"

Notice that these people recognize that God is with the converted Jews, but there is no mention of God being in them. They will go back to Jerusalem, hoping and pleading for God's grace, but to no avail.

Isaiah 49:22–23 says,

> This is what the Sovereign LORD says: "See, I will beckon to the Gentiles, I will lift up my banner to the peoples; they will bring your sons in their arms and carry your daughters on their shoulders. Kings will be your foster fathers, and their queens your nursing mothers. They will bow down before you with their faces to the ground; they will lick the dust at your feet. Then you will know that I am the LORD; those who hope in me will not be disappointed."

Some aspects of this prophecy are not fulfilled until the millennial kingdom arrives, and some aspects may be more symbolic than literal.

Believing Jewish Survivors

Now let us look at several verses referencing the ingathering for those who are converted at the end.

First, Isaiah 60:1–5:

> Arise, shine, for your light has come, and the glory of the LORD rises upon you. See, darkness covers the earth and thick darkness is over the peoples, but the LORD rises upon you and his glory appears over you. Nations will come to your light, and kings to the brightness of your dawn. Lift up your eyes and look about you: All assemble and come to you; your sons come from

afar, and your daughters are carried on the arm. Then you will look and be radiant, your heart will throb and swell with joy; the wealth on the seas will be brought to you, to you the riches of the nations will come.

Though these believers are surrounded by God's glory, and are "radiant" and full of "joy," they come with humility. Jeremiah 31:8–9 reads,

See, I will bring them from the land of the north and gather them from the ends of the earth. Among them will be the blind and the lame, expectant mothers and women in labor; a great throng will return. They will come with weeping; they will pray as I bring them back. I will lead them beside streams of water on a level path where they will not stumble, because I am Israel's father, and Ephraim is my firstborn son.

For I will take you out of the nations; I will gather you from all the countries and bring you back into your own land. I will sprinkle clean water on you, and you will be clean; I will cleanse you from all your impurities and from all your idols. I will give you a new heart and put a new spirit in you; I will remove your heart of stone and give you a heart of flesh.

—Ezek. 36:24–26

In Micah 5:3 the prophet wrote, "Therefore Israel will be abandoned until the time when she who is in labor gives birth and the rest of his brothers return to join the Israelites." They return after "Jacob's trouble" and the second coming of Christ. (See also Isa. 49:5–6; 60:3–4; Zech. 8:8.)

Finally Israel will no longer be symbolized as a barren woman; the labor of the tribulation is over and she is fertile again. The prophecy in Galatians 4:27, a paraphrase of Isaiah 54:1, will finally be fulfilled: "Be glad, O barren woman, who bears no children; break forth and cry aloud, you who have no labor pains; because more are the children of the desolate woman than of her who has a husband." The woman with the husband represents the "law," but the desolate woman finally has a husband in the "grace of Christ."

The prophecy in Isaiah 27:6 will also come true: "In days to come Jacob will take root, Israel will bud and blossom and fill all the world with fruit."

Isaiah 49:17–21 says,

> "Your sons hasten back, and those who laid you waste depart from you. Lift up your eyes and look around; all your sons gather and come to you. As surely as I live," declares the LORD, "you will wear them all as ornaments; you will put them on, like a bride.

> "Though you were ruined and made desolate and your land laid waste, now you will be too small for your people, and those who devoured you will be far away. The children born during your bereavement will yet say in your hearing, 'This place is too small for us; give us more space to live in.' Then you will say in your heart, 'Who bore me these? I was bereaved and barren; I was exiled and rejected. Who brought these up? I was left all alone, but these—where have they come from?'"

Jerusalem is "desolate" and in "bereavement" at the time of the second coming of Christ, but Israel's sons return at the ingathering. The children born to her are saved away from Israel in Bozrah, and other places throughout the world. The saved Jewish people return at the ingathering, and their numbers are so large that Jerusalem cannot hold them during the millennium kingdom.

Chapter 27

The millennial kingdom of Christ will be a time unlike any other in the history of the world. God will create a new heaven and a new earth. Satan will be bound for a thousand years in the Abyss (hades) (Rev. 20:1–3), and the raptured saints will have glorified bodies and will be in heaven that is attached to earth at Mount Zion. While this chapter is not intended to be a comprehensive study of the millennium, let's look at a few interesting highlights of this exciting period.

Timing

What is a little confusing about the book of Revelation, as I've stated previously, is that it is not completely linear. Many chapters begin with the word *then* instead of *and*, which is the more accurate interpretation from the Greek. Therefore, many who read Revelation assume when they read the word "Then" that the succeeding paragraphs or chapters relate events chronologically. Such potential for confusion exists in the transition for Revelation 20 to 21, in which the great white throne judgment seems to immediately precede the creation of the new heaven and new earth. In reality, however, the new creation occurs prior to the beginning of the millennial kingdom—a thousand years before the great white throne.

For further clarity as to the exact timing of the creation of the new heaven and new earth, we need to look at Isaiah 66:20–24:

"And they will bring all your brothers, from all the nations, to my holy mountain in Jerusalem. . . . And I will select some of them also to be priests and Levites," says the LORD.

"As the new heavens and the new earth that I make will endure before me," declares the LORD, "so will your name and descendants endure. From one New Moon to another and from one Sabbath to another, all mankind will come and bow down before me," says the LORD. "And they will go out and look upon the dead bodies of those who rebelled against me; their worm will not die, nor will their fire be quenched, and they will be loathsome to all mankind."

In this passage we learn that the new heaven and new earth will be associated with the Sabbath and New Moon celebrations during the millennial kingdom, where people will travel to Jerusalem to bow down before the Lord and give tithes and offerings.

Second Peter 3:10, 13 states, "But the day of the Lord will come like a thief. The heavens will disappear with a roar; the elements will be destroyed by fire, and the earth and everything in it will be laid bare. . . . But in keeping with his promise we are looking forward to a new heaven and a new earth, the home of righteousness." According to these verses, it appears that the new heavens and earth are created after the second coming of Christ and his judgments that burn up the earth.

Then in Hebrews 12:26–28 we read, "At that time his voice shook the earth, but now he has promised, 'Once more I will shake not only the earth but also the heavens.'" The words *once more* indicate the removing of what can be shaken—that is, created things—so what cannot be shaken may remain. What remains after the tribulation is the new heaven and new earth, which cannot be shaken. (See Isa. 65:17, 20; Matt. 24:35; Zech. 14:8–10.)

The New Heaven

Heaven will be elevated, but attached to earth at Mount Zion. Revelation 21:10–21 says the new heaven will be a cube, extending up from Mount Zion. Each side of the cube is approximately 1,400 miles, which is certainly large enough to house all the converted saints throughout all history.

Christ will be at the throne, and we will rule the earth with him.

- "I saw thrones on which were seated those who had been given authority to judge. And I saw the souls of those who had been beheaded because of their testimony for Jesus and because of the word of God" (Rev. 20:4).
- "Do you not know that the saints will judge the world?" (1 Cor. 6:2).
- "Jesus said to them, 'I tell you the truth, at the renewal of all things, when the Son of Man sits on his glorious throne, you who have followed me will also sit on twelve thrones, judging the twelve tribes of Israel. And everyone who has left houses or brothers or sisters or father or mother or children or fields for my sake will receive a hundred times as much and will inherit eternal life'" (Matt. 19:28–29).

The New Earth

After God finishes judging the earth, every mountain and island will be removed (Rev. 16:20), so the new earth will be relatively flat and probably a single landmass, as it was before the great flood of Noah's time—a latter-day Pangaea, if you will. The only elevated area will be at Mount Zion, according to Isaiah 2:2: "In the last days the mountain of the LORD's temple will be established as chief among the mountains; it will be raised above the hills, and all nations will stream to it." And Zechariah 14:8–10 states,

> On that day, living water will flow out from Jerusalem,
> half to the eastern sea and half to the western sea, in
> summer and in winter.

> The LORD will be king over the whole earth. On that day there will be one LORD, and his name the only name.

> The whole land from Geba to Rimmon, south of Jerusalem, will become like the Arabah [a flat plain], but Jerusalem will be raised up and remain in its place.
> (See also Isa. 11:9; Ezek. 40:2; Mic. 4:1)

The earthly millennial temple area will extend out from Christ's footstool on Mount Zion. Such a temple is described in explicit detail in Ezekiel 40–41. So the Most Holy Place in the millennial temple is where Christ's feet are positioned (although some may question whether this is figurative or literal in interpretation).

During the millennium, the truly saved people will travel intermittently to offer tithes to God at Mount Zion. In Micah 4:2–3 we read,

> Many nations will come and say, "Come, let us go up to the mountain of the LORD, to the house of the God of Jacob. He will teach us his ways, so that we may walk in his paths." The law will go out from Zion, the word of the LORD from Jerusalem. He will judge between many peoples and will settle disputes for strong nations far and wide.

Evidently, the highways leading to Mount Zion will be elevated, and only the redeemed will be able to use them. Isaiah 35:8–10 says, "And a highway will be there; it will be called the Way of Holiness. The unclean will not journey on it; it will be for those who walk in that Way. . . . But only the redeemed will walk there, and the ransomed of the LORD will return." (See also Isa. 51:11.) Isaiah 49:11 states, "I will turn all my mountains into roads, and my highways will be raised up." (See also Isa. 11:16; 19:23.)

Joel 2 describes what is actually happening with the creation of the new earth. Angels of God who look like "locusts" (Joel 2:4–11) refurbish the earth and create a garden of Eden setting. (See also Isa. 57:3; Ezek. 36:34.) Verse 3 (KJV) says, "A fire devoureth before them; and behind them a flame burneth: the land is as the garden of Eden before them, and behind them a desolate wilderness; yea, and nothing shall escape them." No material thing is left unaffected by the locusts, which appear to be moving backward. Verse 11 says, "The LORD thunders at the head of his army; his forces are beyond number, and mighty are those who obey his command." Also, it appears that the survivors of the tribulation actually witness the new creation process by these locust armies. Verse 6 reads, "At the sight of them, nations are in anguish; every face turns pale." The survivors from Israel are called to repent during this process (Joel 1:13–14; 2:12–14), and when the locusts have finished their mission, "I will pour out my Spirit on all people. Your sons and daughters will prophesy, your old men will dream dreams, your young men will see visions" (Joel 2:28). It is most likely that the angelic locust invasion occurs within the seventh bowl judgment.

The statement in Revelation 21:1, "no longer any sea," should not be taken to mean there will be no bodies of water in the new creation. This is supported by Ezekiel 47:8–9a, 12:

> He said to me, "This water flows toward the eastern region and goes down into the Arabah, where it enters the Sea. When it empties into the Sea, the water there becomes fresh. Swarms of living creatures will live wherever the river flows. . . . Fruit trees of all kinds will grow on both banks of the river. Their leaves will not wither, nor will their fruit fail. Every month they will bear, because the water from the sanctuary flows to them. Their fruit will serve for food and their leaves for healing."

The "sea" in Revelation 21:1 is a metaphor for the rebellion and sin of humankind, which will be removed when the new order is achieved in the eternal state.

Aging in the Millennium

Because the unsaved cannot go to the "living water" during the millennial kingdom, some will die. The fact that there is a need for living water during the millennial kingdom and that some people die during this period refutes those who do not believe in a thousand-year, literal millennial kingdom, but claim that the "eternal state" occurs after the second coming of Christ.

Isaiah 65:20 says, "Never again will there be in it an infant who lives but a few days, or an old man who does not live out his years; he who dies at a hundred will be thought a mere youth; he who fails to reach a hundred will be considered accursed." The conditions during the millennium will be like that of the garden of Eden. Remember, before the flood (Gen. 6), people lived hundreds of years—and that's after sin entered humanity. The genealogy in Genesis 5 gives examples of people living seven, eight, and nine centuries. The oldest man on record, Methuselah, lived to 969 years of age!

The classic reference to the millennial kingdom is found in Isaiah 11:6–8:

> The wolf will live with the lamb, the leopard will lie down with the goat, the calf and the lion and the yearling together; and a little child will lead them. The cow will feed with the bear, their young will lie down together, and the lion will eat straw like the ox. The infant will play near the hole of the cobra, and the young child put his hand into the viper's nest.

The animals do not seem to be carnivores any longer, and nature seems to be in perfect harmony. (See also Hos. 2:18.) Notice that there are children and infants, and probably adults of varying ages, which also clearly disproves this being the "eternal state," as there is no sin or aging in the "eternal state."

Messianic Jews in the Millennium

The converted Jews have a privileged position during the millennial kingdom. Isaiah 49:23 says, "Kings will be your foster fathers, and their queens your nursing mothers. They will bow down before you with their faces to the ground; they will lick the dust at your feet." Even if we don't interpret the verse literally, it's clear that Gentiles will hold the Jewish people in high regard during the millennium kingdom, and will serve them and show them honor and deference. Isaiah 62:12 says the Jews will be "sought after."

Not only will they be honored, the Jewish people will be a nation of priests in the millennial kingdom. Isaiah 61:5–6 states, "Aliens will shepherd your flocks; foreigners will work your fields and vineyards. And you will be called priests of the LORD." And Exodus 19:6 reads, "'you will be for me [God] a kingdom of priests and a holy nation.' These are the words you are to speak to the Israelites."

Though the Jews in the millennial kingdom are served by the Gentile world, it still appears that the Jews will do some work. Ezekiel 39:7–16 states,

> I will make known my holy name among my people Israel. I will no longer let my holy name be profaned, and the nations will know that I the LORD am the Holy One in Israel. It is coming! It will surely take place, declares the Sovereign LORD. This is the day I have spoken of.
>
> Then those who live in the towns of Israel will go out and use the weapons for fuel and burn them up—the small and large shields, the bows and arrows, the war clubs and spears. For seven years they will use them for fuel. They will not need to gather wood from the fields or cut it from the forests, because they will use the weapons for fuel. And they will plunder those who plundered them and loot those who looted them, declares the Sovereign LORD.
>
> On that day I will give Gog a burial place in Israel, in the valley of those who travel east toward the Sea. It will block the way of travelers, because Gog and all his hordes will be buried there. So it will be called the Valley of Hamon Gog.
>
> For seven months the house of Israel will be burying them in order to cleanse the land. All the people of the

land will bury them, and the day I am glorified will be a memorable day for them, declares the Sovereign LORD.

Men will be regularly employed to cleanse the land. Some will go throughout the land and, in addition to them, others will bury those that remain on the ground. At the end of the seven months they will begin their search. As they go through the land and one of them sees a human bone, he will set up a marker beside it until the gravediggers have buried it in the Valley of Hamon Gog. (Also a town called Hamonah will be there.) And so they will cleanse the land.

One may question why the Jews will be burying those bodies during the millennial kingdom. Didn't God create new heavens and a new earth at the end of the tribulation? Isaiah 66:24 states, "And they will go out and look upon the dead bodies of those who rebelled against me; their worm will not die, nor will their fire be quenched, and they will be loathsome to all mankind." It appears that God keeps the site of the battle of Armageddon as a memorial for those during the millennial kingdom and as a reminder of the wages of sin and the ultimate destiny of those who reject Christ.

Peace in the Kingdom

The millennial kingdom is associated with true world peace.

- "Bow and sword and battle I will abolish from the land, so that all may lie down in safety" (Hos. 2:18b).
- "He will proclaim peace to the nations. His rule will extend from sea to sea and from the River to the ends of the earth" (Zech. 9:10b).
- "He makes wars cease to the ends of the earth; he breaks the bow and shatters the spear, he burns the shields with fire" (Ps. 46:9).

- "He will judge between many peoples and will settle disputes for strong nations far and wide. They will beat their swords into plowshares and their spears into pruning hooks" (Mic. 4:3).

So not all the weapons will be burned up, as in the Valley of Armageddon; some will be used for farming.

Abundant Provision in the Kingdom

Farming in the millennial kingdom will be the greatest the world has ever seen, excluding the garden of Eden. Amos 9:11–14 says,

> "In that day I will restore David's fallen tent. I will repair its broken places, restore its ruins, and build it as it used to be, so that they may possess the remnant of Edom and all the nations that bear my name," declares the LORD who will do these things.
>
> "The days are coming," declares the LORD, "when the reaper will be overtaken by the plowman and the planter by the one treading grapes. New wine will drip from the mountains and flow from all the hills. I will bring back my exiled people Israel."

This passage indicates that there will be a continual harvest of crops during the millennium.

Malachi 3:11–12 states, "'I will prevent pests from devouring your crops, and the vines in your fields will not cast their fruit,' says the LORD Almighty. 'Then all the nations will call you blessed, for yours will be a delightful land,' says the LORD Almighty." Zechariah 14:6 says there will be "no cold or frost."

The millennial kingdom will not only be associated with an abundance of physical food, but there will be an abundance of spiritual food throughout the world. Habakkuk 2:14 says, "The earth will be filled with the knowledge of the glory of the LORD, as the waters cover the sea." (See Isa. 11:9.)

Chapter 28

The Jewish temple sacrificial system will be implemented during the millennial kingdom, but the sacrifices will *not* be for the remission of sins. Jesus will be dwelling in the temple. Unlike the prior Old Testament temple worship, all will be worshiping God in faith, in spirit, and in truth. Going to the temple to worship will help the mortals recognize their sin, as Ezekiel 43:10 states: "Son of man, describe the temple to the people of Israel, that they may be ashamed of their sins." Hopefully they will come away with a deeper appreciation of how great Jesus is, having repented of their sins, and having gained power for righteous living.

Sun and Moon

God promised that as long as the sun's and moon's rotations around the earth have not permanently ceased, if there is a descendant from David on the throne, there will also be a temple worship system of Levites and priests.

> "In those days and at that time I will make a righteous Branch sprout from David's line; he will do what is just and right in the land. In those days Judah will be saved and Jerusalem will live in safety. This is the name by which it will be called: The LORD Our Righteousness." For this is what the LORD says: "David will never fail to have a man to sit on the throne of the house

of Israel, nor will the priests, who are Levites, ever fail to have a man to stand before me continually to offer burnt offerings, to burn grain offerings and to present sacrifices."

The word of the LORD came to Jeremiah: "This is what the LORD says: 'If you can break my covenant with the day and my covenant with the night, so that day and night no longer come at their appointed time, then my covenant with David my servant—and my covenant with the Levites who are priests ministering before me—can be broken and David will no longer have a descendant to reign on his throne.'"

—Jer. 33:15–21

Since Jesus is on the throne during the millennial kingdom and the sun and moon are still rotating, there must be temple worship for the Word of God to be true. There has not been a continuous kingship of David's lineage or a continuous temple worship system due to the sin and rebellion of the people. (See Jer. 36:30.) But whenever a descendent from David is on the throne in Israel there will always be sacrificial temple worship—as long as the sun and moon are rotating.

We know from Scripture that the covenant God has with the sun and moon will end when the eternal state begins, at the end of the millennial kingdom. Isaiah 60:18b–22 says,

"You will call your walls Salvation and your gates Praise. The sun will no more be your light by day, nor will the brightness of the moon shine on you, for the LORD will be your everlasting light, and your God will be your glory. Your sun will never set again, and your moon will wane no more; the LORD will be your everlasting light, and your days of sorrow will end. Then will all your people be righteous."

The sun and moon will not disappear in the eternal state, but will stop rotating and their light will not affect the earth, because the glory of God will completely overpower them. Revelation 22:3–5 says,

No longer will there be any curse. The throne of God and of the Lamb will be in the city, and his servants will serve him. They will see his face, and his name will be on their foreheads. There will be no more night. They will not need the light of a lamp or the light of the sun, for the Lord God will give them light. And they will reign for ever and ever.

An Obsolete System?

Many biblical scholars may argue against the prophecies about millennial kingdom sacrifices by claiming that Christ's death on the cross made the old sacrificial systems obsolete. They quote Hebrews 8:13: "By calling this covenant 'new,' he has made the first one obsolete; and what is obsolete and aging will soon disappear." The new covenant discussed here is with the house of Israel when God "will put [his] laws in their minds and write them on their hearts" (Heb. 8:10). This prophecy will be fulfilled in the end-times revival of Israel, when they go from a "salvation by works" mentality, to a "salvation by grace through faith" system. This sacrificial system and associated "old covenant" is now "obsolete" in that Christ's death was the ultimate payment for sin, yet the requirement of the "old covenant" will not disappear for the Jewish people until the eternal state is reached. Saying otherwise creates a contradiction in Scripture. Certainly Ezekiel 40–48, which describes the millennial temple in explicit detail, cannot be a figment of the prophet's imagination.

The "old covenant" is clearly tied to the earthly sanctuary/temple worship system according to Hebrews 9:1: "Now the first covenant had regulations for worship and also an earthly sanctuary." Verses 2–7 talk about specifics of the "Most Holy Place" and how the high priest went in once a year to offer blood for the sins of the people. Then verses 8–10 say,

> The Holy Spirit was showing by this that the way into the Most Holy Place had not yet been disclosed as long as the first tabernacle was still standing. This is an illustration for the present time, indicating that the

gifts and sacrifices being offered were not able to clear the conscience of the worshiper. They are only a matter of food and drink and various ceremonial washings—external regulations applying until the time of the new order.

An earthly tabernacle existed from the time of Moses until the time of Solomon, who built the first temple. (See Ex. 25:8–40; 38:21; Num. 1:50; 17:7; 1 Kings 6–8.) That temple was destroyed and rebuilt several times until its permanent destruction in A.D. 70. During the tribulation a temple will be constructed again (Rev. 11:1–2). Acts 7:44–50 discusses how inferior these earthly tabernacles and temples are compared with God's final tabernacle, which will not be built with human hands. The heavenly tabernacle will be on Mount Zion at the second coming of Christ. This is also consistent with the discussion in Hebrews 9:11–14.

The New Order

So the sacrificial Jewish system is required until the "new order" is in place (Heb. 9:10). The Greek word used for "new order" here is used only once in Scripture, and it means "to straighten thoroughly or restore to its original condition from that which was broken." The eternal state corresponds to this definition of new order, because there will be no more sin or illness or death, and our broken earthly tabernacles will be replaced by our heavenly tabernacle. (See 2 Cor. 5:1–4; 2 Peter 1:13.) Revelation 21:4 says, "There will be no more death or mourning or crying or pain, for the old order of things has passed away." This verse clearly shows that the new order starts in the eternal state. Hebrews 9:15 says, "For this reason Christ is the mediator of a new covenant, that those who are called may receive the promised eternal inheritance—now that he has died as a ransom to set them free from the sins committed under the first covenant." So the ultimate fulfillment of the "new covenant" occurs once we arrive at the eternal state, when we will indeed be totally free from sin and clothed with our heavenly attire. Though we are in the dispensation of the new covenant now, the ultimate fulfillment is in the eternal state.

The implementation of the "new covenant" requires the "blood of Jesus" and is fully implemented in our individual lives after we die or at the rapture, whichever comes first. Hebrews 9:17–23 states:

> This is why even the first covenant was not put into effect without blood. When Moses had proclaimed every commandment of the law to all the people, he took the blood of calves, together with water, scarlet wool and branches of hyssop, and sprinkled the scroll and all the people. He said, "This is the blood of the covenant, which God has commanded you to keep." In the same way, he sprinkled with the blood both the tabernacle and everything used in its ceremonies. In fact, the law requires that nearly everything be cleansed with blood, and without the shedding of blood there is no forgiveness.
>
> It was necessary, then, for the copies of the heavenly things to be purified with these sacrifices, but the heavenly things themselves with better sacrifices than these.

Though we have been crucified with Christ and are dead to sin (Gal. 2:20) at our conversion, we still have to deal with our "sin nature" until the new covenant is fully realized at our death or rapture.

During the millennial kingdom, the temple sacrifices will be a form of worship offered in faith and will point back to the ultimate sacrifice for sin that occurred with Christ Jesus at the crucifixion. Hebrews 10:1, 3–4 states,

> The law is only a shadow of the good things that are coming—not the realities themselves. For this reason it can never, by the same sacrifices repeated endlessly year after year, make perfect those who draw near to worship. . . . But those sacrifices are an annual reminder of sins, because it is impossible for the blood of bulls and goats to take away sins.

Certainly, the animal sacrifices can never take away sin, but they are a good "reminder of sins." As the millennial worshipers pass by the valley of Armageddon and see those whose "worm" is in hell, they will also have a reminder of sin and the need to evangelize the lost (Isa. 66:24). As celebration of the Lord's Supper by the New Testament church (1 Cor. 11:25) is done regularly to commemorate Christ's death, so the millennial mortals will offer animal sacrifices in a like manner, though Christ has already died for us and them.

Hebrews 10:18 says, "And where these have been forgiven, there is no longer any sacrifice *for sin.*" This verse does not say that there is no longer any sacrifice needed, but no longer any sacrifice for sin needed. The New Testament Gentile saints are not called to animal sacrifices, but we are called to continually offer up our bodies as "living sacrifices holy and pleasing to God," which is our "spiritual act of worship" (Rom. 12:1). We are also to "offer to God a sacrifice of praise—the fruit of lips that confess his name" (Heb. 13:15).

Jeremiah 3:16–17

Some refute the possibility of a sacrificial system being implemented in the millennial kingdom by quoting Jeremiah 3:16–17a:

> "In those days, when your numbers have increased greatly in the land" declares the LORD, "men will no longer say, 'The ark of the covenant of the LORD.' It will never enter their minds or be remembered; it will not be missed, nor will another one be made. At that time they will call Jerusalem The Throne of the LORD, and all nations will gather in Jerusalem to honor the name of the LORD."

However, Revelation 11:19a states, "Then God's temple in heaven was opened, and within his temple was seen the ark of his covenant." The ark symbolizes the Old Testament sacrificial system, but Jesus himself will replace the ark in the millennial temple. There is no mention at all in the millennial temple discussions in Ezekiel 40–48 of the ark of the covenant, but this does not mean the temple sacrificial system has been done away with. The fact that the "ark" terminology is used in Revelation gives us some clues that there will be some representation of the old sacrificial system in the end times. (See also Heb. 9:4; Ex. 25:10–22; 2 Chron. 5:7.)

Revelation 15:5 says, "After this I looked and in heaven the temple, that is, the tabernacle of the Testimony, was opened."

Here again, we see another end times reference to a symbol that is central to the Old Testament sacrificial system, "the tabernacle of the Testimony." (See also Ex. 38:21; Num. 1:50, 53; 9:15; 10:11.)

More Details?

One may ask why Revelation does not give a more detailed description of the millennial temple worship system, as in Ezekiel 40–48. The answer to this question becomes evident when one considers that in the book of Revelation, the emphasis is on the end-times Gentile believers who will be raptured at the second coming of Christ. They are not going to participate in this sacrificial system, since they will be in the eternal state at the time it is again implemented. Ezekiel, on the other hand, lived and wrote during the time of the old sacrificial system of the Jewish state, and his emphasis for the end times is from the Jewish perspective. Incidentally, the book of Hebrews emphasizes the old sacrificial system because that book was primarily written to Jewish converts to Christ. (See also Isa. 56:6–8; 66:21–23; Ezek. 20:40–41; Zech. 14:16–21; Mal. 3:2–4.)

Priests in the Kingdom

The millennial kingdom will have both heavenly and earthly priests. (Remember, heaven is attached to earth at Mount Zion at this point.)

The Heavenly Priests

The heavenly priests are mentioned in Revelation 5:9b–10, which states, "with your blood you purchased men for God from every tribe and language and people and nation. You have made them to be a kingdom and priests to serve our God, and they will reign on the earth." So the raptured saints will be the heavenly priesthood that will reign during the millennium kingdom, and they will be instruments of righteousness. They will judge sin like Phinehas (Num. 25), who—as a lesson to Israel—drove a spear through an Israelite who was fornicating with a Midianite woman, thereby stopping the plague that killed 24,000. Revelation 20:6 also references the raptured saints: "Blessed and holy are those who have part in the first resurrection. The second death has no power over them, but they will be priests of God and of Christ and will reign with him for a thousand years." (See also Rev. 1:6; 2:26; 1 Cor. 4:8; 6:2; 1 Peter 2:9; Matt. 25:21–23; Luke 19:17, 19; 2 Tim. 2:12.)

Each raptured saint will have a different region of authority throughout the world, and those whose lives exemplified greater levels of obedience and self-sacrifice will have greater levels of authority and greater glory in the millennial kingdom. Also, Luke 22:28–30 states, "I confer on you a kingdom, just as my Father conferred one on me, so that you may eat and drink at my table in my kingdom and sit on thrones, judging the twelve tribes of Israel."

The Earthly Priests

There are two groups of earthly millennial priests: the "sons of Zadok" and everybody else. The sons of Zadok are honored because their ancestors did not fall into idol worship during the time of Adonijah's rebellion with the priest Abiathar. (See 1 Kings 1; Ezek. 44:10–16.) They are the only priests able to offer sacrifices—burnt offerings and sin offerings (Ezek. 43:18–27)—and "draw near to the LORD to minister before him" (Ezek. 40:46).

Though the priests of Zadok are able to get close to the Lord, I don't believe they will be able to see Jesus in all his glory and still live as mortals—and they are clearly mortals.

> They must not shave their heads or let their hair grow long, but they are to keep the hair of their heads trimmed. No priest is to drink wine when he enters the inner court. They must not marry widows or divorced women; they may marry only virgins of Israelite descent or widows of priests. They are to teach my people the

difference between the holy and the common and show them how to distinguish between the unclean and the clean.

In any dispute, the priests are to serve as judges and decide it according to my ordinances. They are to keep my laws and my decrees for all my appointed feasts, and they are to keep my Sabbaths holy.

A priest must not defile himself by going near a dead person. . . . On the day he goes into the inner court of the sanctuary to minister in the sanctuary, he is to offer a sin offering for himself, declares the Sovereign LORD.

—Ezek. 44:20–25, 27

Notice that these priests are limited to judging issues related to the temple and other religious matters. They do not have the greater authority that the raptured saints have as judges of civil matters in the millennial kingdom. (See also Ezek. 40:38–47; 42:1–20.)

Our Great High Priest and Prince

Discussion of the millennial temple would not be complete without mention of the position of the Prince.

My servant David will be king over them, and they will all have one shepherd. They will follow my laws and be careful to keep my decrees. They will live in the land I gave to my servant Jacob, and the land where your fathers lived. They and their children and their children's children will live there forever, and David my servant will be their prince forever. I will make a covenant of peace with them; it will be an everlasting covenant. I will establish them and increase their numbers, and I will put my sanctuary among them forever. My dwelling place will be with them; I will be their God, and they will be my people. Then the nations will know that I the LORD make Israel holy, when my sanctuary is among them forever.

—Ezek. 37:24–28

Then in Ezekiel 34:23–24 we read, "I will place over them one shepherd, my servant David, and he will tend them; he will tend them and be their shepherd. I the LORD will be their God, and my servant David will be prince among them. I the LORD have spoken."

Though some believe these passages refer to King David in raptured form, I believe the Prince is the Great Shepherd Jesus, who is in the lineage of David. (See also Ps. 89:4–5; Zech. 6:12–13; Dan. 8:28; Matt. 2:6; Acts 5:31.)

Jesus is not the only prince mentioned, however. There are other princes in the temple.

Mortal Princes

Ezekiel 44:1–3 states,

> Then the man brought me back to the outer gate of the sanctuary, the one facing east, and it was shut. The LORD said to me, "This gate is to remain shut. It must not be opened; no one may enter through it. It is to remain shut because the LORD, the God of Israel, has entered through it. The prince himself is the only one who may sit inside the gateway to eat in the presence of the LORD. He is to enter by way of the portico of the gateway and go out the same way."

The Prince holds an honored position, as only he may enter through the east gate, which was closed once Christ entered the temple, and he will sit and "eat in the presence of the LORD." It is hard for me to imagine that any mortal could do that and continue to live to talk about it. However, Exodus 24:9–11 (italics added) says, "Moses and Aaron, Nadab and Abihu, and the seventy elders of Israel went up and saw the God of Israel. *Under his feet* was something like a pavement made of sapphire, clear as the sky itself. But God did not raise his hand against these leaders of the Israelites; they saw God, and they ate and drank." My conclusion is that they did not see the full glory of Jesus, but just his feet. In this way, the princes in the millennial temple will be able to sit and eat with Jesus, and still live to talk about it.

So the mortal princes for the millennial kingdom are the leaders of Israel. They are analogous to the elders who ate with God. Micah 3:1 (KJV) says, "And I said, Hear, I pray you, O heads of Jacob, and ye princes of the house of Israel; Is it not for you to know judgment?" Unlike some of the past leaders of Israel,

> My princes will no longer oppress my people but will allow the house of Israel to possess the land according to their tribes.
>
> This is what the Sovereign LORD says: You have gone far enough, O princes of Israel! Give up your violence and oppression and do what is just and right. Stop dispossessing my people, declares the Sovereign LORD. You are to use accurate scales, and accurate ephah, and an accurate bath.
>
> —Ezek. 45:8b–10

The princes will receive offertory gifts from the mortals in the millennial kingdom. They will be able to keep many of the gifts, but will provide one sixth to one tenth as sacrificial offerings for atonement for the sins of the people at the New Moons and Sabbaths, as well as all appointed feasts. (See Ezek. 45:1–46:24.) So it appears that they offer sacrifices only on the special days, and the priests take care of the sacrifices on all other days. Princes receive land bordering the sacred district and the property of the city Jerusalem (Ezek. 45:7), and they may give gifts to their sons and descendants (Ezek. 46:16–18).

Raptured saints, unlike the princes eating at the feet of Jesus during the millennial kingdom, will often eat at table level with the glory of God. Since they will have glorified bodies, they will be able to see the full glory of God. After Jesus remarked on the great faith of the centurion, he said, "I tell you the truth, I have not found anyone in Israel with such great faith. I say to you that many will come from the east and the west, and will take their places at the feast with Abraham, Isaac and Jacob in the kingdom of heaven" (Matt. 8:10–11; see also Matt. 22:1–14; Luke 13:24–29; 22:16–18; Isa. 49:12; 55:1; Zech. 14:16–19).

Chapter 21

After the millennium kingdom ends and the final war is won (Rev. 20:7–10), the great white throne judgment of unbelievers takes place. Then the mortal saints are glorified, and judged. Ultimately, the eternal state occurs when heaven comes down to earth proper. It's interesting to note that there is no reference to these mortal believers after the end of the millennium ever facing death or being raptured. It's assumed that they are instantly glorified while on the earth, but we don't have much detail in Scripture on that.

The new order and the eternal state are described in Revelation 21:2–7:

> I saw the Holy City, the new Jerusalem, coming down out of heaven from God, prepared as a bride beautifully dressed for her husband. And I heard a loud voice from the throne saying, "Now the dwelling of God is with men, and he will live with them. They will be his people, and God himself will be with them and be their God. He will wipe every tear from their eyes. There will be no more death or mourning or crying or pain, for the old order of things has passed away."
>
> He who was seated on the throne said, "I am making everything new!" Then he said, "Write this down, for these words are trustworthy and true."

> He said to me: "It is done. I am the Alpha and the
> Omega, the Beginning and the End. To him who is
> thirsty I will give to drink without cost from the spring
> of the water of life. He who overcomes will inherit all
> this, and I will be his God and he will be my son."

Christ's footstool will be on Mount Zion and his feet will be in the Most Holy Place of the millennial temple, as we discussed in chapter 27. At that time heaven will be elevated, yet connected to the earth at Zion. But once the eternal state begins, heaven, the "new Jerusalem," will descend to the level of the earth, and will replace the earthly Jerusalem and the temple site. There will be no more death or mourning, and the whole world will see God in all his glory. God will indeed be living with everyone, and all will be glorified in the eternal state. We will literally "inherit the earth" (Rev. 21:7; Matt. 5:5) when heaven comes down. This earthly Jerusalem and temple area is much smaller than the heavenly throne and the New Jerusalem, so they are clearly two separate entities. (See Ezek. 48:30–35 and compare with Rev. 21:15–24.)

The statement "I am making everything new" (Rev. 21:5) refers to the new order, whereby sin, mourning, and death are done away with. The earthly city of Jerusalem is also made new, but I believe the emphasis is on the new order and not the fact that the new heaven and new earth were created, since this would have been done a thousand years earlier.

Revelation 21:9–21 is a bit of a flashback, but discussion of the eternal state picks up again at verses 22–23: "I did not see a temple in the city, because the Lord God Almighty and the Lamb are its temple. The city does not need the sun or the moon to shine on it, for the glory of God gives it light, and the Lamb is its lamp." So the millennial temple is gone in this scene, which is of the eternal state, because sin and death have ceased.

The river of life still appears to be present in the eternal state, but instead of flowing out from under the millennial temple, it will be flowing from the throne of God in the middle of the great street in the New Jerusalem.

Then the angel showed me the river of the water of life, as clear as crystal, flowing from the throne of God and of the Lamb down the middle of the great street of the city. On each side of the river stood the tree of life, bearing twelve crops of fruit, yielding its fruit every month. And the leaves of the tree are for the healing of the nations. No longer will there be any curse. The throne of God and of the Lamb will be in the city, and his servants will serve him. They will see his face, and his name will be on their foreheads. There will be no more night. They will not need the light of a lamp or the light of the sun, for the Lord God will give them light. And they will reign for ever and ever.

—Rev. 22:1–5 (see also Zech. 14:8)

Notice that we may not be at "eternal rest" in the eternal state, since we will be serving him. (See also Rev. 7:15.) Oh, what a privilege to serve our Lord forever and ever!

POSTSCRIPT WHAT SHOULD WE DO TO PREPARE FOR CHRIST'S RETURN?

In response to the plethora of information on the last days that we have been inundated with, Christians in America need to emulate the church members at Berea (Acts 17:11), who compared what was preached to what the Scriptures actually had to say on the subject. We need to seek the truth, above our own personal preferences. I do admit that study of the end times requires more than a superficial check of Scripture, largely because of the deception that has been taught to us through the pulpits and Christian radio and books, making it even more difficult to find the truth on this issue. To arrive at the proper paradigm, we must be willing to look at all viewpoints of the rapture and end-times events, and then analyze all applicable Bible verses, praying that God, through the Holy Spirit, will reveal the truth. That said, I believe a rational unbiased approach to this subject, as supported by this book, will remove any doubt on this issue of whether the church will be here for much of the tribulation.

Since the Day of Pentecost, when the Holy Spirit was given to believers, the church has faced periods of extreme persecution. This didn't come as a surprise to early believers, nor should it to us in the twenty-first century. The Bible tells us to expect it:

- "If they persecuted me, they will persecute you also" (John 15:20b).
- "In fact, everyone who wants to live a godly life in Christ Jesus will be persecuted" (2 Tim. 3:12).

- "In this you greatly rejoice, though now for a little while you may have had to suffer grief in all kinds of trials. These have come so that your faith—of greater worth than gold, which perishes even though refined by fire—may be proved genuine and may result in praise, glory and honor when Jesus Christ is revealed" (1 Pet. 1:6–7).

Regarding persecution in the last days, 2 Timothy 3:1 says, "But mark this: There will be terrible times in the last days"; and Matthew 24:21 states, "For then there will be great distress, unequaled from the beginning of the world until now—and never to be equaled again."

Most people who have studied the end times, independent of their rapture viewpoint, believe that we are on the brink of the tribulation. Yes, believers in Christ for the last two thousand years have thought the return of Christ would occur in their generation. But they did not see the fulfillment of all the Bible prophecies related to the nation Israel, as we have seen in recent times. Also, it seems likely that terrorists will soon obtain nuclear weapons, and once that happens, they will likely try to exterminate Israel with one blast. God will not allow that to happen, so he will intercede. He will return!

The times are right for America to step out of the way as a superpower, and for the revised Roman Empire and the Antichrist to ultimately emerge. America is certainly due for its "day of reckoning." How patient God must be with America! Prayer has been taken out of schools, millions of babies have been aborted, and unbelievable forms of sexual immorality have been exploited here and exported throughout the world. The television has become the great tool of Satan. Money and military power are now what this nation puts its trust in instead of God. Most churches in America are like the churches of Sardis or Laodicea, at best. As James 5:5 says, we have indeed "lived on earth in luxury and self-indulgence." America, we have indeed "fattened" ourselves for "the day of slaughter."

First Response

So what should we do with this changed paradigm we now have of anticipating that we may be entering the tribulation soon? The first thing to do is to make sure Jesus is your personal Lord and Savior. Have "you confess[ed] with your mouth, 'Jesus is Lord,' and believe[d] in your heart that God raised him from the dead" (Rom. 10:9)? Is your life changed by your confession of faith (2 Cor. 5:17)? Are you attending church regularly? Do you have a hunger for reading God's Word daily and praying daily? Is Jesus the absolute ruler of your life? If not, I implore you to put this book down now and make things right between you and God. He loves you and wants you to come to him in humility and gratitude.

Experiencing Blessing

If you know your life is in order before God, then Revelation 1:3 applies to you: "Blessed is the one who reads the words of this prophecy, and blessed are those who hear it and take to heart what is written in it, because the time is near." But how? Could it be that by knowing God's end-times plan we would have time to get our hearts ready and make preparations for the perilous times ahead? Through the help of the book of Revelation, we should be able to recognize the false powers of the Antichrist, the Beast, and the False Prophet, and know how to avoid the "mark." One could certainly see how most of today's Christians would be demoralized and severely question their faith if they found themselves unexpectedly in the tribulation. Fortunately some Christians today, like the Bereans, challenge what is preached in their churches. These Christians who know the truth were prophesied about in Daniel 11:32b–33: "the people who know their God will firmly resist him [the Antichrist]. Those who are wise will instruct many, though for a time they will fall by the sword or be burned or captured or plundered." These Christians will be called to preach the truth and help strengthen the brethren when their faith is severely challenged. Daniel 12:3 states, "Those who are wise will shine like the brightness of the heavens, and those who lead many to righteousness, like the stars for ever and ever." I don't know about you, but I'd like to be known as one of these "wise" Christians, who will have greater glory in the judgment, because we did not stumble in the tribulation, but were a source of wisdom for the end-times saints.

The "Starry Host"

Daniel 8:10–14 talks about the "starry host," who will not fare so well in the end times. Verse 10 says, "It grew [the Antichrist] until it reached the host of the heavens, and it threw some of the starry host down to the earth and trampled on them." Then in verse 13b we read of "the rebellion that causes desolation, and the surrender of the sanctuary and of the host that will be trampled underfoot." Some believe the "starry host" is a reference to the fallen angels that were cast to the earth, but I disagree. The Antichrist would not trample on his partners in crime (demons). Besides, the fallen angels were knocked down to the earth long before the Antichrist will gain power. The Hebrew word used for "starry host" means a "mass of persons." I contend that they are God's elect, some of which are deceived by the Antichrist and False Prophet. The Hebrew word for "trampled" means "abasement or state of spiritual compromise." This starry host will still have eternal life, but they lose much of their eternal reward. (See Matt. 24:24; Dan. 11:35; Heb. 10:37–39; 2 John 8; also Phil. 2:15.)

A seemingly similar passage refers to the fall of one third of the angels in heaven, prior to the incarnation of Jesus: "Then another sign appeared in heaven: an enormous red dragon with seven heads and ten horns and seven crowns on his heads. His tail swept a third of the stars out of the sky and flung them to the earth" (Rev. 12:3–4). The Greek word for "star" or "aster" used here represents celestial bodies, however, not humans.

Jesus said, "For false christs and false prophets will appear and perform great signs and miracles to deceive even the elect—if that were possible. See, I have told you ahead of time" (Matt. 24:24–25). The popular preaching on this verse today is that it will not be possible for the elect to be deceived, but why would Jesus mention it if it were not possible? Jesus was emphasizing that not only will the unsaved be deceived, but even some of the elect, as hard as that would be to imagine.

We don't want to be part of the starry host who are trampled on by Satan, because of spiritual compromise. We need to have the impetus to finish the course, as the apostle Paul desired to do, so that we "will not be disqualified for the prize" (1 Cor. 9:27).

Self-Imposed Captivity

Once we know the truth about the end-times prophecies, we must ask the question: Could God be calling some to self-imposed captivity? Hebrews 11:38 says, "the world was not worthy of them. They wandered in deserts and mountains, and in caves and holes in the ground." We must remember that Hebrews 11 is devoted to men and women of faith throughout history, but could it not also apply to the end-times church believers? Would it be out of character for God to start and end the church age with similar conditions for his people? Could he be calling some Christians to live in small communities where finances and talents are pooled, as in the days of the early church in Acts?

We have many biblical examples where people of God were called to flee into self-imposed captivity: Lot and his family (Gen. 19:16–18); Jacob (Gen. 27:41); Moses (Ex. 2:11); David (1 Sam. 22–24); the one hundred prophets concealed by Obadiah (1 Kings 18:3–4); Joseph, Mary, and Jesus (Matt. 1:18–24); Paul (2 Cor. 11:33).

David had a hard time understanding God's call for him to flee.

> In the LORD I take refuge. How then can you say to me: "Flee like a bird to your mountain. For look, the wicked bend their bows; they set their arrows against the strings to shoot from the shadows at the upright in heart. When the foundations are being destroyed, what can the righteous do?"

> The LORD is in his holy temple; the LORD is on his heavenly throne. He observes the sons of men; his eyes examine them. The LORD examines the righteous.
> —Ps. 11:1–5a

The world was falling apart around David, which is what the tribulation saints will encounter as well. Though their ultimate trust is in God and they have assurance of his eyes being on them, they will still need to act as birds and flee. Proverbs 28:12 states, "When the righteous triumph, there is great elation, but when the wicked rise to power, men go into hiding." When the Antichrist comes to ultimate power in the middle of the tribulation, will not many be called to flee?

Several verses appear to be specific guidance for Jews in the tribulation. Matthew 24:15–21; Mark 13:9–20; and Luke 12:8–12 tell the Jews in Judea at the time of the abomination of desolation to flee to the mountains. Certainly, the same instruction should also apply to Gentile believers at the abomination.

Jesus also makes reference to the end-times Jews who don't flee to the mountains, but remain in Israel (Matt. 10:17–23). Their own family members and other fellow Jews will turn them in. Likewise, I believe this same fate will be shared by many Gentiles who don't flee the last Babylon after the abomination of desolation. Matthew 10:23 commands, "When you are persecuted in one place, flee to another. I tell you the truth, you will not finish going through the cities of Israel before the Son of Man comes."

Jesus is also the one speaking in Revelation 18:4 when he calls all saints to "Come out of her, my people, so that you will not share in her sins, so that you will not receive any of her plagues." The general call here is for all to flee the last Babylon that is set up during the later half of the tribulation period. Zechariah 2:7 states, "Come, O Zion! Escape, you who live in the Daughter of Babylon."

Several Old Testament passages, especially in Jeremiah, instructed the Israelites on how they were to respond to the initial Babylonian invasion. Maybe some of these same verses give us useful insights for the end-times saints who will have to deal with the last Babylon.

- "Furthermore, tell the people, 'This is what the LORD says: See, I am setting before you the way of life and the way of death. Whoever stays in this city will die by the sword, famine or plague. But whoever goes out and surrenders to the Babylonians who are besieging you will live; he will escape with his life'" (Jer. 21:8–9). These verses appear to give each person a choice in his or her ultimate destiny against the Babylonians. In this situation, however, self-imposed captivity was not an option.
- "Flee for safety, people of Benjamin! Flee from Jerusalem!" (Jer. 6:1).
- "Do not go out to the fields or walk on the roads, for the enemy has a sword, and there is terror on every side" (Jer. 6:25).

Jeremiah 15:2 says, "Those destined for death, to death; those for the sword, to the sword; those for starvation, to starvation; those for captivity, to captivity." Some may say that the tribulation saints have a similar destiny and that their actions will not affect the outcome. But this view contradicts Jeremiah 21:8–9, where there appears to be a choice. Also, the word *destined* in Jeremiah 15:2 has been added, and the Hebrew Scriptures have no equivalent word that is used.

The most specific guidance for Gentile saints in the tribulation is found in Revelation 13:9–10: "He who has an ear, let him hear. If anyone is to go into captivity, into captivity he will go. If anyone is to be killed with the sword, with the sword he will be killed. This calls for patient endurance and faithfulness on the part of the saints." It appears that there are two fates for the elect during the tribulation—either captivity or being killed. Some biblical scholars erroneously interpret these verses to say that they refer to the Antichrist's enemy forces, implying that God will repay those who kill by later having them killed, and those who bring Christians into captivity will ultimately be put into captivity. This is not true. All the forces of the Antichrist have the same fate: death in the battle of Armageddon and eternal damnation in the lake of fire.

As God uses the words "He who has an ear, let him hear" (verse 9), he sets before us the knowledge of the future and commands his people to listen and take to heart what he says. The wise should give heed to his warnings and be delivered through faith in the word of God. In verse 10, the Greek word for "go"—*sunago*—means to lead with one's self or to lead together or collect or to lead together or assemble to a resort or refuge. Thus the captivity option seems to include self-imposed captivity, which will give the end-times saints some influence over their earthly outcomes during the tribulation. Of course, our decisions should be based on what we hear God calling us specifically to do. But, from these verses, it seems clear that we are not to resist or fight back with the weapons of this world.

Those who know the end-times prophecies should see the option of self-imposed captivity in the call to flee Babylon. Those who refuse to believe the truth, or have a greater love for this world than for spiritual things, will likely be too late for this option to flee. Their choice will be either to take the mark of the Beast or face severe persecution, prison, and death. I'd rather face these options knowing this was God's specific calling for me than to have them forced on me due to a series of wrong choices on my part because of spiritual ignorance and/or carnality.

Without Excuse

Those who refuse to believe the tribulation truths will have no excuse. Daniel 11 says the wise will instruct many people in the truth about the end times, yet many of the saints "will fall by the sword or be burned or captured or plundered" (Dan. 11:33). Evidently, many still reject the truth and do not try to flee the last Babylon, despite being warned by the wise in adequate detail. Verses 34–35 state, "When they fall, they will receive a little help, and many who are not sincere will join them. Some of the wise will stumble, so that they may be refined, purified and made spotless until the time of the end, for it will still come at the appointed time." Those saints who fall spiritually into compromise will receive help from deceivers. (See Matt. 7:15; Rom. 16:18.) The "wise" who "stumble" do not spiritually stumble, as the translation implies, but they just "fall by the sword" or are "captured" or "burned" in a self-sacrificial way. It is not the "wise" who need to be "refined, purified and made spotless," but the compromising apostate church members. Some of the wise will have already exited the last Babylon, but will return to help those apostate tribulation saints recognize these false prophets. Fortunately, many ignorant tribulation saints will finally recognize the error of their ways and stop the compromise. The verse above implies that these apostates who finally repent get martyred for their faith, since this is the only way to be made "spotless until the time of the end." At this point in time, it would probably be impossible to flee the last Babylon. The end referenced in Daniel 12:13 is the day of rapture, in regard to those who have already died and "rest" in heaven until they are glorified on the "last day."

James 5

The entire fifth chapter of James seems to be a most specific prophetic reference to those living on earth during the last days. Verses 1–5 describe rich people hoarding wealth and fattening themselves for the day of slaughter that will occur at the second coming of Christ. Then verses 7–20 discuss the last days from the perspective of the saints. We should be patient in waiting for the Lord's coming and should be willing to suffer and persevere and pray for our fellow saints. Verse 20 says, "remember this: Whoever turns a sinner from the error of his way will save him from death and cover over a multitude of sins." Could it be that the "wise" of the last days (Dan. 11:33–35) will instruct other believers of the need to flee Babylon, so that they won't wander from the faith and be killed by the world's systems? Could it be that those heeding the instruction of the wise might avoid being killed "by the sword or be burned or captured or plundered"? Are not many Christians in America hoarding wealth that will ultimately be plundered by this world? Should they not be the ones giving more to charity at this time and making plans for an underground church support system? Will not most tribulation saints be required to show they "Do not love the world or anything in the world?" (1 John 2:15–29).

Focus on Your Family

Another argument for self-imposed captivity is found in the God-ordained calling given to spiritual leaders of families. These patriarchs are to do their best to provide protection for their families, and this requirement will not change during the tribulation. In those days, many women will be taken captive, raped, and severely beaten. Zechariah 14 gives one example of the women of Israel suffering in this manner near the end of the tribulation. Many people will even be decapitated for the faith. Shouldn't family leaders have an exodus plan for their loved ones? Yes, there are times God will call families to take severe risks for a specific mission he has for them, and God is the ultimate protector. There will be some whom God will call specifically to be martyrs or to be imprisoned for the faith, but Scripture does not support a general calling for all the end-times saints to suffer this fate; it seems to be the exception rather than the rule.

I believe it may be prudent to have a place of refuge established for our families—and perhaps others—through the tribulation. Even if God calls you individually, when the time comes, to be put in prison or martyred for Christ, you will have still taken care of your loved ones.

Certainly, we should not use such preparations to become isolationists, and we should not flee the last Babylon prematurely. We should also not allow preparations for a place of refuge to affect our mission to evangelize or to limit our giving to charitable causes. In fact, the last days should compel us even more to give, rather than save for some retirement program. We should be even more impassioned to evangelize the lost, because the time is indeed short.

Martyrdom

While there's nothing wrong with pursuing the option of self-imposed captivity, we must be certain that it is what God is calling us to do.

The highest calling of the church is to evangelize the world (Matt. 28:19–20), and Jesus said that he would be with us to the "end of the ages," providing the power we need to carry out his command—even during the tribulation. If we look at church history we see that often the witness from the death of martyrs becomes the seed for future church growth. Paul witnessed Stephen's stoning (Acts 7) and became the greatest preacher and writer in Christian history. The death of Polycarp later in the first century resulted in three thousand new converts to Christ. That's how we magnify our witness. Hebrews 11:35 says, "Others were tortured and refused to be released, so that they might gain a better resurrection." Paul wrote, "To live is Christ and to die is gain" (Phil. 1:21), and Jesus said, "Whoever finds his life will lose it, and whoever loses his life for my sake will find it" (Matt. 10:39).

Several verses in Revelation highlight a call to martyrdom for some tribulation saints.

- "Be faithful, even to the point of death, and I will give you the crown of life" (Rev. 2:10b).
- Those martyred for the faith are also mentioned in Revelation 6:10–11, where they ask God to avenge their blood. In response, "they were told to wait a little longer, until the number of their fellow servants and brothers who were to be killed as they had been was completed." So there are a specific number of saints who are called to be martyrs, and God knows who they are.

- "They overcame him by the blood of the Lamb and by the word of their testimony; they did not love their lives so much as to shrink from death" (Rev. 12:11).
- "This calls for patient endurance on the part of the saints who obey God's commandments and remain faithful to Jesus. Then I heard a voice from heaven say, 'Write: Blessed are the dead who die in the Lord from now on'" (Rev. 14:12–13).

Revelation 20:4 says those "beheaded for their testimony" will be given greater authority to rule during the millennial kingdom. If you do not feel the calling to be a tribulation martyr for Christ and you flee the last Babylon to a place of refuge, you should be prepared mentally and spiritually to keep the faith whatever the cost—arrest, prison, torture, or even death—knowing that the Holy Spirit will enable and empower you to make the right choice.

Certainly, some of the saints living during the time of the tribulation will be called to die for their faith, but this will not be the norm. The references to the "multitude" of saints in heaven (Rev. 7:9; 19:1–15) who were raptured out of the tribulation show no evidence of martyrdom. Revelation 15:2 says the raptured saints are "those who had been victorious over the beast and his image and over the number of his name." Not all who are raptured require martyrdom for the victory. Those who are in self-imposed captivity are also victorious over the Beast, and are still threatened with death during most of the tribulation because they could be discovered any minute and killed.

I see the rationale both for and against self-imposed captivity. I can see some saints being led by God to remain in the mainstream cultures until they are imprisoned or martyred for their faith, which will probably be in the latter half of the tribulation. It does appear, however, that most saints in the tribulation will be called to flee the last Babylon. Hopefully, most will have the discernment to not only know the end-times scriptures, but will also know specifically what God wants them to do. John 16:13 says, "But when he, the Spirit of truth, comes, he will guide you into all truth. He will not speak on his own; he will speak only what he hears, and he will tell you what is yet to come." I'm afraid, however, that many Christians will be ignorant of the end-times scriptures, and will compromise their faith, because they will not be physically, spiritually, or psychologically prepared for what is to come.

As the end times loom ever closer, the saints will be told more and more. Perhaps this is why Marvin Rosenthal, Robert Van Kampen, and Hank Hanegraaff have recently written books refuting a pretribulation rapture. Amos 3:7 states, "Surely the Sovereign LORD does nothing without revealing his plan to his servants the prophets." Though Jesus is the last prophet, it would not be inconsistent with God to reveal his end-times prophecies and plan to those Christians who diligently seek the truth about his Word and walk by the Spirit.

It does appear that some of the end-times prophecies have been sealed (Dan. 8:26) until the last days unfold. The prophet Daniel had firsthand experience of seeing prophecies unsealed. While he was reading the writings of Jeremiah, he discovered that the Babylonian captivity would end in seventy years. Knowing this, he was able to help the Jewish people prepare for their return to Israel. Though I make no claim to be a prophet, some of these prophecies have recently opened up to me, as well, though I have read them multiple times in the past and had no clear understanding until more recently. There should be clearer revelation for many more believers once the tribulation actually begins. When Christians with faulty end-times paradigms experience the persecution that is heading their way, hopefully then they will finally understand the truth.

Whatever you decide to do regarding the end times, you need to realize that Jesus will keep you strong to the end if your focus is on him. We don't need to be overwhelmed with fear or be overly focused on searching for the Antichrist or other signs, but our focus should be on Jesus. One thing is for certain: The church is not going to be raptured before the tribulation begins. Our mind-set should be one of expecting persecution, and we should be instructing others against the end-times church deception that is so prevalent in America today. Such deception feeds into what Satan has planned for this world and will enhance the great "falling away" that will be manifested by many church attendees in the last days. We should definitely live with a sense of urgency and stronger commitment to Christ Jesus. We should be bold in our witness. What an amazing thought that we could be the last Christians to finish the church age! Our focus should not be in just surviving the tribulation, but in glorifying and magnifying our Lord and Savior, Jesus Christ, the only true God. We shall overcome! His name is to be forever praised! Amen!

The 144,000 Jewish evanglists are converted near the start of the tribulation, the peace treaty is signed by Antichrist and many nations.

Day 220 begins the sacrifice at the Jewish temple with the cornerstone being laid. There are 2,300 days until the second coming of Christ.

Month 1	2-7	8	9-11	12	13	14-24

The first seal is opened at the start of the tribulation as Antichrist rides the white horse.

The second seal/red horse begins as Antichrist rides the terrorist movement (start time after first seal unknown).

The first three trumpets occur sometime within the first half of tribulation period, with manifestations of the third trumpet, or Wormwood, lasting throughout.

Universal religious system ("great prostitute) starts near the beginning of the tribulation period and falls around two weeks prior to the abomination.

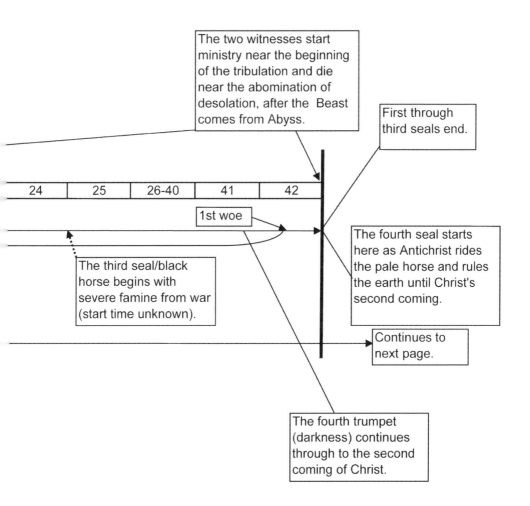

The two witnesses start ministry near the beginning of the tribulation and die near the abomination of desolation, after the Beast comes from Abyss.

First through third seals end.

| 24 | 25 | 26-40 | 41 | 42 |

1st woe

The third seal/black horse begins with severe famine from war (start time unknown).

The fourth seal starts here as Antichrist rides the pale horse and rules the earth until Christ's second coming.

Continues to next page.

The fourth trumpet (darkness) continues through to the second coming of Christ.

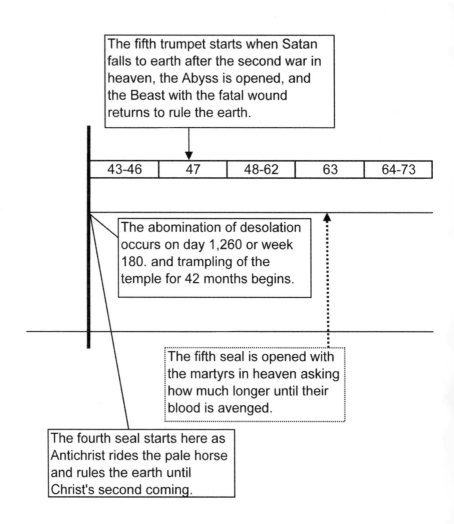

The fifth trumpet starts when Satan falls to earth after the second war in heaven, the Abyss is opened, and the Beast with the fatal wound returns to rule the earth.

| 43-46 | 47 | 48-62 | 63 | 64-73 |

The abomination of desolation occurs on day 1,260 or week 180. and trampling of the temple for 42 months begins.

The fifth seal is opened with the martyrs in heaven asking how much longer until their blood is avenged.

The fourth seal starts here as Antichrist rides the pale horse and rules the earth until Christ's second coming.

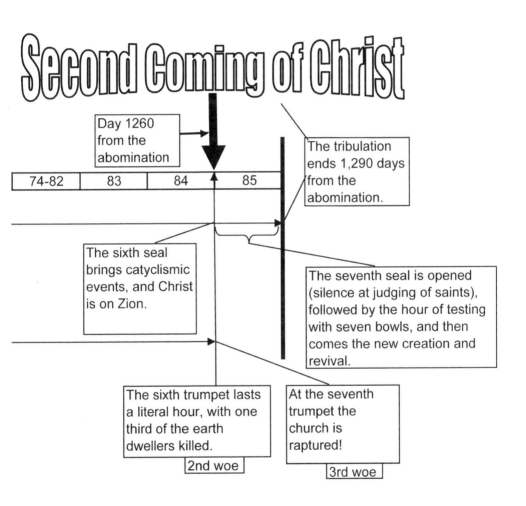